BREAKING BREAD

with FATHER DOMINIC

D1053633

FATHER DOMINIC GARRAMONE, OSB

First Edition
Second Printing

ISBN 0-9674652-0-6

Printed in the United States of America by Inland Press/Inland Book, Menomonee Falls, Wisconsin.

KETC
3655 Olive St.
St. Louis, MO 63108

Visit the *Breaking Bread With Father Dominic* Web site at *http://www.breaking-bread.com*. Instructional videotapes from the *Breaking Bread With Father Dominic* television program may be ordered at 1-800-293-5949.

Breaking Bread With Father Dominic is underwritten by Fleischmann's Yeast and Hodgson Mill.

TABLE OF CONTENTS

TABLE OF CONTENTS

Editor:
Terri Gates

Designer:
Beth Hasek

Recipe editor:
Barbara Gibbs Ostmann

Illustrator:
Michael Neville

Cover photo:
Scott Raffe

"Cum omni humilitate faciant ipses artes."

(Rule of St. Benedict 57:1)

About the Author

Father Dominic Garramone is a Benedictine monk at St. Bede Abbey in Peru, a small town in northern Illinois. He has been kneading for fun and fellowship ever since he baked his first baguette as a grade school project in Peoria, Illinois—and he's never stopped. He welcomes friends to the abbey's kitchen whenever he bakes, whether to help him create a new bread, learn some of his bread making secrets, or simply to sample his latest loaf fresh out of the oven. At least once a week Father Dom rolls up the sleeves of his monk's habit to plunge into the next batch of dough. "One of the problems, of course, is that white flour on a black habit is really noticeable!" he says with a smile.

He enjoys researching breads of foreign cultures to help him develop new recipes, and says he's also inspired by the variety of flavors grown in his herb garden. Among the recipes in this book, Father Dominic says that Apricot Skillet Bread evolved spontaneously from ingredients he found in the abbey refrigerator one day, and the impromptu recipe required no tweaking after it emerged from the oven. On the other hand, he recalls that Sourdough Onion Rye Bread and Papa Dom's Pizza Topping needed many trial runs before the recipes were honed to his satisfaction.

Father Dominic entered the monastery in 1983 when he was 22 years old. He is chairman of the religion department for St. Bede Academy, the coed prep school run by the monastery, plus he teaches freshman religion, and directs theater productions for high school and grade school students. He graduated summa cum laude from St. Mary's College in Winona, Minnesota, and earned two Master's degrees, also summa cum laude, from St. Meinrad School of Theology in southern Indiana.

Articles about bread baking and herb gardening by Father Dominic have been published in magazines *The Healthy Planet* and *Potpourri From Herbal Acres*. His children's play, *The Monsters Under the Bed*, was published in 1997 by Dramatic Publishing, Inc.

Introduction

I had my first experience of bread baking when I was in fifth grade. For a class project I had to make some kind of ethnic food, and my mother, an experienced baker, said, "Make French bread—that's easy." So I learned the basics of bread baking, and turned out two beautiful baguettes, which I proudly took to class along with some unsalted butter and apricot preserves. My classmates were enthusiastic in their praise, and it was gratifying to see them enjoying what I had made. They devoured every crumb, and I felt a real sense of accomplishment.

This treasured memory has formed the pattern for all my subsequent years of baking. With each new recipe I have learned something, and enjoyed the accompanying feeling of achievement. Whether I was baking for the cast of my high school play or my college dorm buddies or my fellow monks in the abbey, bread has been a means of expressing affection and fostering fellowship. Today, nothing makes me happier than seeing a freshly baked loaf of my bread disappear at the lunch table.

To bake bread is to invite fellowship, as can be clearly seen in the etymology of the word "companion": "with" + "bread." We share our bread with our companions on life's journey. It's almost impossible to bake homemade bread and eat it alone. The aroma of freshly baked bread always entices people to gather in the kitchen, and before long, you've got an impromptu party!

As a monk, I have a great love for tradition, and that includes baking traditions. To be a baker is to become part of a rich history of culture, to tap into the diversity of human creativity and celebration that is in danger of being lost in the modern age. Almost every ethnic group has its unique bread, with names that form a litany that tease the imagination as well as the palate: limpa, nisu, gugelhupf, fougasse, povitica, ekmek, panettone, hoska, challah. Baking these breads brings a fulfillment to both body and spirit.

I would like you to have the same fulfilling experience of baking. Baking bread is easier than you think. You don't have to worry about absolutely perfect measurement of ingredients, it doesn't require special equipment and the dough can be left alone for literally hours at a time without coming to harm. Like I tell people when I'm teaching baking: "It's bread—it's going to forgive you!"

The pages that follow will introduce you to the basics of bread baking, while the recipes offer a sampler of the world of breads. By becoming a baker, you'll find that you are feeding your senses as well as your family and friends. Savor the aroma of yeast and herbs, caress the lively texture of the dough as you knead, feel the flush of fragrant steam when you open the oven. Your soul will be nourished and renewed, even before you take the first bite.

ABOUT FLOURS

Bread dough rises because bubbles of carbon dioxide produced by the yeast are trapped by stretchy strands of gluten (a protein molecule in the flour), resulting in expansion of the dough. White wheat flour contains the most gluten and is most commonly used in bread baking. Whole wheat flour has slightly less gluten than wheat flour; rye and barley have less yet; and cornmeal, millet, soy and buckwheat have hardly any. Flours with the least gluten should be added to the dough only in small amounts (no more than one cup per loaf), while medium gluten flours (such as whole wheat and rye) can make up about half the flour in the dough.

In my experience, the best flour for bread is unbleached white bread flour. Bread flour is made from a harder variety of wheat grain, so it holds up better under the process of kneading and rising, and it has a higher percentage of gluten than all-purpose flour, which is made from a combination of hard and soft wheat. Doughs made with bread flour sometimes require more kneading to develop the gluten. Bread flour is especially good in sourdough recipes.

Having said that, however, I don't want to give the impression that you can't make good bread from all-purpose flour. You can, and if that's what you have in the house, go ahead and use it—you'll still get a good result. But with the revival of bread making in recent years, many more flours are available at the average grocery store. So the next time you're shopping, spend some time in the flour aisle and see what's available in your area.

ABOUT YEAST

Yeast is a microorganism that feeds on the natural sugars in flour, producing carbon dioxide in the process. The bubbles produced within the dough are what causes bread to rise. Because yeast is a living organism, care must be taken to provide an appropriate environment for it. The most common mistake novice bakers make is to kill the yeast by using too-hot liquid. The optimal range of temperature for promoting the growth of the yeast is between 100 and 110 degrees. When you're first learning to bake bread, it's a good idea to check the temperature of the liquids with an instant-read thermometer (easily obtained wherever cooking utensils are sold). In a pinch, a good rule of thumb is to think of yeast as a baby—the liquid should be about the same temperature as baby formula.

Yeast comes in several forms: active dry, cake yeast, instant, sourdough, etc. While some recipes in this book use baking powder, baking soda or sourdough for leavening, most of the recipes have been carefully developed and tested for active dry yeast. Yeast in this form comes in foil envelopes (three envelopes joined together) with each envelope holding about 2 1/4 teaspoons of yeast. Active dry yeast also comes in larger bags or jars. Check the back of the package for the expiration date—yeast that is too old will not rise properly. Also, be sure to follow the directions in each recipe carefully to ensure consistent results.

ABOUT OTHER INGREDIENTS

Bread recipes include other ingredients in various proportions, each of them making a unique contribution to the dough:

Liquids: The liquid in bread may be anything from water to milk to tomato juice to beer. The first time you try a recipe, use the liquid that is specified before experimenting with other choices. Once you become proficient, you can begin to create your own variations. Be sure to use a measuring cup specifically designed to measure liquids (as opposed to a dry measure). Otherwise, your proportions will be affected.

Salt: The addition of salt to a recipe isn't only for flavor—it also helps control the rate of fermentation, strengthens the gluten network, and adds to the shelf life of the bread.

Sugar: Sugar helps the fermentation process by giving the yeast an additional source of food. It also adds flavor and helps bread develop a rich brown crust. Granulated sugar, brown sugar, molasses and honey are all used in bread baking.

Fats and Oils: Most bread recipes call for some kind of enriching ingredient like oil, butter or shortening. Some may also call for eggs (unless otherwise specified, use large eggs). Enriched breads have a softer, more tender crumb, and keep longer. Use the enriching ingredients specified for each recipe whenever possible—any substitution is bound to change the character of the dough.

ABOUT EQUIPMENT

Everything you need for making basic bread is probably in your kitchen right now: a large mixing bowl, measuring cups (both dry and liquid), measuring spoons, a sturdy wooden spoon, a clean dish towel, an oven, some kind of wire rack for cooling the bread once it's baked, and loaf pans or heavy-gauge baking sheet. I prefer a heavy baking sheet with four sides (also called a jelly-roll pan) rather than a cookie sheet, which is a lighter sheet of metal with a lip on only one side. Using insulated baking or cookie sheets will affect baking times. Other useful tools include:

cutting board	razor blade or sharp knife
pastry brush	kitchen timer
flour sifter	rolling pin
pastry blender	oven thermometer
instant-read thermometer	water sprayer or atomizer

Be sure to read the recipe carefully before beginning a baking project, to make sure you have all the necessary tools.

ABOUT MIXING

In each recipe, follow the directions carefully regarding the order in which the ingredients are mixed, and the length of time to stir until the next ingredient is added. This is especially important when adding flour to the dough; if you add too much flour at a time, the result will be a lumpy dough with an uneven crumb.

You'll notice that in many recipes, the amount of flour is variable. The moisture and protein content of flours vary greatly from season to season, and sometimes even from sack to sack. Thus, the amount of flour needed for a recipe may also vary every time you make it. On a humid day, the dough may also absorb moisture from the air, which will affect the amount of flour used as well. With most bread dough it is better to err on the sticky side—too much flour will result in a dry, crumbly bread.

About Kneading

The process of kneading is what develops the gluten network of the dough that traps the carbon dioxide produced by the yeast and causes the dough to rise. So good kneading is essential to the character of the dough. Begin with the slightly flattened dough on a lightly floured counter in front of you. Take hold of the edge farthest from you and fold the dough toward you, pulling the dough back on itself. Using the heels of your hands, push the dough away from you in a rolling motion. Turn the dough one quarter and then repeat. This three-step process—fold, push, turn—will gradually become a smooth, rhythmic process. Most yeast breads are kneaded from 6 to 8 minutes, sometimes longer. After kneading, the dough is usually oiled lightly and placed back in the rinsed mixing bowl to rise.

About Rising

Most (but not all) yeast breads have two periods of rising: the first rising in the bowl and the second rising after the loaves are shaped. In both cases the environment in which the rising dough is kept is crucial. A warm place free from drafts (75 to 85 degrees) is preferred. Follow the directions in each recipe for specific times for each rising. As a general rule, the first rising takes 1 to 2 hours, or until the dough is doubled in bulk. If you're not sure if the dough has doubled, use the fingertip test. Insert your finger in the center of the risen dough; if the hole does not fill in immediately, the dough is ready for shaping. After the loaves are shaped, the second rising takes about half the time of the first rising. Again, follow the directions for each individual recipe regarding the timing on this second rising.

ABOUT BAKING

Each oven has its own peculiarities, so it may take several baking trials before you get used to how yours works. Some ovens are hotter at the back of the oven than the front, or may be cooler near the bottom of the oven. If you have uneven heat in your oven, turn the pan halfway through the baking process. The oven's thermostat may not be entirely accurate, especially on older models, so you may want to invest in a good oven thermometer so you can test yours. Unless the recipe tells you otherwise, always preheat your oven to the recommended temperature before placing the loaves in for baking.

You'll notice that most recipes give you a range for baking times (e.g., 45 to 55 minutes). The type and size of the oven, the material of the baking pan, the humidity in the kitchen, and many other factors can affect how long it takes for bread to be done. One time-honored test for doneness is to thump the bottom of the loaf after removing it from the pan; if it sounds hollow, it's done. (Underdone bread often sticks to the pan.) If it's been removed too early, it can be put back into the pan immediately and returned to the oven for more baking.

Once the bread comes out of the oven, it is actually still baking, so resist the temptation (which will be considerable!) to cut into the loaf immediately. If you wait 20 minutes or so before slicing, the bread will still be warm but will not be doughy on the inside. Moisture from the center of the loaf works its way outward during the cooling period, so always cool your freshly baked loaves on wire racks or the bottom crust will get soggy. Wait until the bread cools completely before storing it in a cloth or plastic bread bag.

ABOUT THIS BOOK

I love the wonderfully tactile nature of bread baking, so I generally urge people to make bread the old-fashioned way and get their hands in the dough. But I also realize that bread machines can be a blessing for people who are short on time. So wherever possible, this cookbook includes a bread machine version of recipes for those who prefer that method.

Look for the 〔Bread Machine〕 symbol, and make sure you're using the appropriate recipe. While the ingredients will be similar for the two versions, the amounts will be quite different.

Basic Breads

Basic White Bread

Yield: 2 loaves.

Bread Break

This is my mother's basic white bread recipe. She won her first blue ribbon for this bread at the Peoria Heart of Illinois Fair in 1967, and has won first prize five times since then. (Her raisin bread has won ribbons 21 times.) I've made this bread so often, I don't even need the recipe anymore.

2 cups warm **water**

2 packages **FLEISCHMANN'S Active Dry Yeast**

2 tablespoons **granulated sugar**

2 teaspoons **salt**

¼ cup **vegetable oil**

6 to 6½ cups **HODGSON MILL Best for Bread Flour**, divided

Put water in a large bowl. Add yeast; stir to dissolve. Let stand 5 to 10 minutes, or until foamy. Add sugar, salt and oil; stir to mix. One cup at a time, add 5 cups of the flour, mixing thoroughly each time. By hand, work in enough of remaining flour to make a soft dough. Turn out onto lightly floured surface and knead 6 to 8 minutes, or until smooth and elastic.

Place dough in large, oiled bowl and turn to coat. Cover bowl with a clean towel. Let rise in a warm, draft-free place about one hour, or until doubled in bulk. Punch dough down.

Divide dough into two equal pieces and form each piece into a loaf. Place in greased 9x5x3-inch loaf pans. Cover and let rise about 45 minutes, or until nearly doubled.

Bake on lower shelf of a preheated 400-degree oven about 35 minutes, or until top is golden brown and bread sounds hollow when lightly tapped. Remove from pans immediately; let cool on wire rack.

≈

Note: You could add 2 tablespoons of any dried herb or herb mixture to this dough to make an herb-flavored loaf.

BASIC WHITE BREAD

Yield: 1 (1 ½-pound) loaf.

1 cup **water**

2 tablespoons **vegetable oil**

1 ½ teaspoons **salt**

3 cups **HODGSON MILL Best for Bread Flour**

1 tablespoon **granulated sugar**

2 teaspoons **FLEISCHMANN'S Bread Machine Yeast**

Add ingredients to bread machine pan in the order suggested by manufacturer. Select **basic cycle; medium/color setting**.

❧

*Note: Use **dough cycle** for other bread machine recipes calling for the basic white dough.*

Yield: About 30 rolls.

Bread Break

I love warm rolls with supper, especially when there's a sauce or gravy to be mopped up. While cloverleaf and bow knots are easier to make, I really prefer the butter fantan. Try all three variations and decide for yourself.

1 package **FLEISCHMANN'S Active Dry Yeast**

$^{1}/_{4}$ cup warm **water**

2 cups **whole milk**

$^{1}/_{4}$ cup ($^{1}/_{2}$ stick) **butter**

2 tablespoons **granulated sugar**

2 teaspoons **salt**

2 **eggs**, beaten

5 to 5 $^{1}/_{2}$ cups **HODGSON MILL Best for Bread Flour** or **Naturally White Flour**, divided

Sprinkle yeast over warm water in small bowl; stir to dissolve. Let stand 5 to 10 minutes, or until foamy.

Heat milk in a saucepan until lukewarm; do not boil. Add butter, sugar and salt; mix well.

Combine milk mixture, yeast mixture and eggs in large bowl of electric mixer fitted with dough hook. Add 2 cups of the flour; mix with dough hook until blended. Add 2 cups flour and mix until blended. Add 1 cup flour and mix on medium speed 2 minutes.

Remove dough from mixing bowl and place on a floured surface. Knead, adding as much of the remaining $^{1}/_{2}$ cup flour as needed to form a smooth, elastic dough. Place dough in a greased bowl and turn to coat. Cover and let rise in a warm, draft-free place 1 to 1 $^{1}/_{2}$ hours, or until doubled.

Punch down dough. Knead 2 minutes to work out air bubbles. Let dough rest 10 minutes. Shape dough into desired rolls. Place on lightly greased baking sheet. Cover and let rise about 30 minutes, or until doubled.

When dough is nearly finished rising, preheat oven to 425 degrees. Bake rolls 15 to 20 minutes, or until golden brown.

SHAPE VARIATIONS

Cloverleaf Rolls: *Lightly grease muffin tins. Roll dough into small, walnut-size balls. Place three balls in each muffin tin. Let rise until doubled in bulk and bake as directed.*

Butter Fantans: *Roll dough into rectangle about ³/₈ inch thick, and brush the top with melted butter. Cut dough into strips about 1¹/₂ inches wide. Stack four strips on top of each other. Cut the strips into individual stacks 2 inches long. Place each stack on end, cut-side down, into greased muffin tins. Cover and let rise until nearly doubled. Bake as directed. Note: Dough may be rolled out thinner and stacked using more layers to fill each muffin cup.*

Bow Knots: *Roll individual pieces of dough into ropes 8 inches to 10 inches long and about ¹/₂ inch thick. Form each rope into a knot, and place on a lightly greased baking sheet. Let rise and bake as directed.*

BASIC ROLLS

Yield: 24 rolls.

¹/₂ cup **water**	3¹/₄ cups **HODGSON MILL Best for Bread Flour**
¹/₂ cup **milk**	
1 **egg**	1 tablespoon plus 1 teaspoon **granulated sugar**
3 tablespoons **butter** or **margarine**	2 teaspoons **FLEISCHMANN'S Bread Machine Yeast**
1¹/₄ teaspoons **salt**	

Add ingredients to bread machine pan in the order suggested by manufacturer. Select **dough/manual cycle**.

When cycle is complete, remove dough from machine to a lightly floured surface. If necessary, knead in enough additional flour to make dough easy to handle. Shape into desired rolls; place on a lightly greased baking sheet. Cover; let rise in warm, draft-free place about 1 hour, or until doubled in size.

Bake in a preheated 425-degree oven 12 to 15 minutes, or until done. Remove from baking sheet; let cool on wire rack.

BASIC WHOLE WHEAT BREAD

Yield: 2 loaves.

Bread Break

A basic whole wheat recipe can be the base for a variety of savory breads, such as Chop Block Bread (page 38). The addition of two or three tablespoons of dried herbs can turn ordinary whole wheat bread into a special accompaniment for your entree.

Although this bread bakes well in loaf pans, I prefer to make round or oval loaves on a baking sheet or baking stone. I use a razor blade to make the classic crisscross slashes in the top of each loaf.

2 cups warm **water**

2 packages **FLEISCHMANN'S Active Dry Yeast**

3 tablespoons **brown sugar**

1 tablespoon **HODGSON MILL Vital Wheat Gluten**

3 cups **HODGSON MILL Whole Wheat Graham Flour**

1/4 cup **vegetable oil**

1 teaspoon **salt**

3 to 3 1/2 cups **HODGSON MILL Best for Bread Flour**, divided

Put water in a large bowl. Add yeast; stir to dissolve. Add brown sugar, gluten and whole wheat flour. Beat well, about 200 strokes. Let yeast develop for about 10 minutes. Add oil and salt; mix thoroughly. Add 2 cups of the bread flour; beat well. Work in enough of the remaining bread flour to form a soft dough.

Turn out onto a lightly floured surface and knead 6 to 8 minutes, or until dough is smooth and elastic. Place in large, oiled bowl and turn to coat. Cover bowl with a clean towel. Let rise in a warm, draft-free place about one hour, or until doubled in bulk.

Punch down dough. Divide dough into two equal pieces and form each piece into a loaf. Place in greased 9x5x3-inch loaf pans. Cover and let rise about 45 minutes, or until nearly doubled.

While dough is rising, preheat oven to 400 degrees. Bake loaves about 35 minutes, or until top is golden brown. Bread is done when it slides easily from the pan and sounds hollow when tapped on the bottom. Let cool on wire racks.

BASIC WHOLE WHEAT BREAD

Yield: 1 (1 1/2-pound) loaf.

1 cup **water**

2 tablespoons **vegetable oil**

1 1/2 teaspoons **salt**

1 1/2 cups **HODGSON MILL Best for Bread Flour**

1 1/2 cups **HODGSON MILL Whole Wheat Graham Flour**

1 1/2 tablespoons **brown sugar**

2 teaspoons **FLEISCHMANN'S Bread Machine Yeast**

1 1/2 teaspoons **HODGSON MILL Vital Wheat Gluten**

Add ingredients to bread machine pan in the order suggested by manufacturer. Select **basic cycle; medium/color setting**.

Note: Use **dough cycle** *for other bread machine recipes calling for the basic whole wheat dough.*

SWEET CORNMEAL MUFFINS

Yield: 12 muffins.

Bread Break

Growing up, I loved corn bread so much I would ask for it instead of cake for my birthday. At my college seminary, we were often served corn bread, lovingly prepared by Sister Stanisia, the seminary cook, who sprinkled the top with sugar before baking to make a sweet, crunchy crust. Now I prefer cornmeal muffins, because they are easier to serve on a buffet. I usually make a double batch of these, putting a dozen in the freezer for future breakfasts or midnight snacks.

1 cup **milk,**
   at room temperature

1 **egg,** beaten

$^1/_4$ cup **solid vegetable shortening,** melted

1 cup **HODGSON MILL Yellow Corn Meal**

$^3/_4$ cup **HODGSON MILL Naturally White Flour**

$^1/_3$ cup **granulated sugar**

3 teaspoons **baking powder**

$^1/_2$ teaspoon **salt**

Preheat oven to 400 degrees.

Combine milk, egg and melted shortening in medium bowl; stir to mix. Place cornmeal, flour, sugar, baking powder and salt in a sifter; sift into the milk mixture. Stir until just blended.

Using a $^1/_4$ cup measure, drop batter into lightly greased muffin tin. Bake 15 to 20 minutes, or until tops of muffins are lightly browned. Let cool slightly. Serve warm.

Note: This is one of the few recipes where I would insist on shortening instead of vegetable oil. There is a noticeable decline in taste with oil, more so than with other breads.

from BREAKFAST TO DESSERT

CARAMEL APPLE CINNAMON ROLLS

Yield: 12 large rolls.

Bread Break

With this recipe you get a breakfast treat that tastes like a cross between a cinnamon roll and a peanut-covered caramel apple — two of my favorite things!

Be sure to use baking apples like Granny Smith, Rome Beauty or Empire—they hold up better during baking and keep their flavor. My absolute favorite baking apple is the Lura Red, but these are not commonly available in supermarkets; check your local apple orchard.

DOUGH:

2 cups **milk**

$^{1}/_{4}$ cup ($^{1}/_{2}$ stick) **butter**

2 tablespoons **granulated sugar**

1 teaspoon **salt**

2 packages **FLEISCHMANN'S Active Dry Yeast**

7 to 7$^{1}/_{2}$ cups **HODGSON MILL Naturally White Flour**, divided

2 **eggs**, beaten

APPLE-CINNAMON FILLING:

$^{1}/_{2}$ cup packed **brown sugar**

$^{1}/_{2}$ cup **granulated sugar**

2 tablespoons **HODGSON MILL Naturally White Flour**

1 $^{1}/_{2}$ tablespoons **ground cinnamon**

$^{1}/_{2}$ cup (1 stick) **butter**, cut into chunks

1 $^{1}/_{2}$ cups chopped, peeled **cooking apple**

1 cup chopped **unsalted, dry-roasted peanuts**

CARAMEL SYRUP:

$^{1}/_{2}$ cup (1 stick) **butter**

1 cup firmly packed **brown sugar**

$^{1}/_{4}$ cup **light corn syrup**

Combine milk, butter, sugar and salt in a medium saucepan. Place over medium heat and stir until mixture is warm and butter begins to melt.

Combine yeast and 2 cups of the flour in a large mixing bowl. Add milk mixture; stir until blended. Add eggs; beat thoroughly, about 200 strokes. Stir in the remaining flour, 1 cup at a time, until you have a cohesive dough. Turn dough out onto a lightly floured surface. Knead about 5 minutes, adding more flour to keep the dough workable, until you have a soft dough that is smooth and elastic.

Rinse the mixing bowl. Grease the surface of the dough and place it in the bowl. Cover with a clean towel and let rise in a warm, draft-free place about 1 hour, or until doubled in bulk.

When the dough is nearly doubled, prepare the filling. Place brown sugar, granulated sugar, flour, cinnamon and butter in a small bowl. Using a pastry blender or two knives, cut butter into sugar mixture until the mixture resembles coarse crumbs.

Set the chopped apple and peanuts aside until you are ready to sprinkle them on the filling.

Punch down dough; knead lightly one minute. Let dough rest while you prepare the caramel syrup. Place butter, brown sugar and corn syrup in a saucepan. Cook over medium heat, stirring constantly, until sugar melts. Remove from heat and set aside until needed.

Roll out dough on a lightly floured surface to a rectangle about 24 by 18 inches. Sprinkle the filling on the dough; top with chopped apple and peanuts. Starting from the long side, roll up jelly-roll style. Pinch the edges to seal. Brush edges of dough with some milk if you have trouble getting the dough to seal.

Evenly pour caramel syrup into a lightly greased 13x9x4-inch baking pan (see note). Using a very sharp knife, cut the dough into 12 pieces. Place pieces, cut-side down, on syrup in pan. Cover and let rise 30 to 45 minutes, or until nearly doubled.

While rolls are rising, preheat oven to 350 degrees. Place a baking sheet on the bottom shelf of the oven to catch any drips. Bake rolls 50 minutes, or until they are lightly browned and sound hollow when tapped. While they are still warm, invert onto a serving plate.

~

Note: *This recipe makes a dozen very large rolls, which requires a deep pan. The standard pan size is 13x9x2 inches; you'll need one that is 13x9x4 inches. If you don't have a pan that deep, or if you want rolls of a more modest size, cut the dough into 18 pieces, use two 9-inch round cake pans and bake 40 to 45 minutes.*

If desired, substitute pecans for peanuts.

Bread Machine

Caramel Apple Cinnamon Rolls

Yield: 12 rolls.

Dough:

1 cup plus 1 tablespoon **milk**

1 **egg**

2 tablespoons **butter**
or **margarine**

$^1/_2$ teaspoon **salt**

3$^1/_2$ cups **HODGSON MILL
Best for Bread Flour**

1 tablespoon **granulated sugar**

2 teaspoons **FLEISCHMANN'S
Bread Machine Yeast**

Apple-Cinnamon Filling:

$^1/_4$ cup ($^1/_2$ stick) **butter**

$^1/_4$ cup firmly packed
brown sugar

$^1/_4$ cup **granulated sugar**

1 tablespoon **HODGSON MILL
Naturally White Flour**

2 teaspoons **ground cinnamon**

$^3/_4$ cup chopped, peeled
cooking apple

$^1/_2$ cup chopped **unsalted, dry-
roasted peanuts** or **pecans**

Caramel Syrup:

$^1/_4$ cup ($^1/_2$ stick) **butter**

$^1/_2$ cup firmly packed
brown sugar

2 tablespoons **light corn
syrup**

Add dough ingredients to bread machine pan in the order suggested by manufacturer. Select **dough/manual cycle**.

While dough is mixing, prepare filling and syrup.

For filling, combine butter, brown sugar and granulated sugar in a medium bowl. With a pastry blender, cut butter into sugars until coarse crumbs form. Stir in flour and cinnamon. Add apple and peanuts; stir to blend. Set aside.

For syrup, combine butter, brown sugar and corn syrup in saucepan. Cook over medium heat, stirring constantly, until sugar melts. Remove from heat. Spread syrup evenly in an ungreased 9-inch square pan. Set aside.

When cycle is complete, remove dough from machine to a

lightly floured surface. If necessary, knead in enough additional flour to make dough easy to handle. Roll to a 12x9-inch rectangle. Spread filling evenly over dough. Beginning from long side of dough, roll up tightly as for a jelly roll. Pinch seam to seal. Cut roll into 12 equal pieces. Place pieces, cut-side down, on syrup in pan. Cover and let rise in warm, draft-free place about 1 hour, or until doubled in size.

Bake in a preheated 350-degree oven 40 to 45 minutes, or until done. While they are still warm, invert onto a serving plate.

Yield: 24 rolls.

Bread Break

These little pastries are really fattening—butter, eggs, sausage—so save them for special occasions and choose something more healthful for your everyday breakfast. My mother makes these almost every year for Christmas brunch, and we devour them. For a breakfast buffet, serve Sausage Roll-Ups on a warming tray, if you have one. If you're the kind of person who pours extra syrup on pancakes so there will be enough to dip your sausage into, try serving these with a little maple syrup drizzled on top.

¹/₄ cup warm **water**

1 package **FLEISCHMANN'S Active Dry Yeast**

1 cup **whole milk**

2 tablespoons **butter**

1 teaspoon **salt**

1 **egg**, lightly beaten

2¹/₂ to 2³/₄ cups **HODGSON MILL Naturally White Flour**, divided

¹/₂ cup (1 stick) **butter**, softened

1 pound bulk **breakfast sausage**, uncooked

Combine water and yeast in a small bowl; stir briefly, then let stand 5 to 10 minutes, or until foamy.

Combine milk and 2 tablespoons butter in a saucepan; warm over medium heat until butter melts. Stir in salt. Let cool to lukewarm.

Pour milk mixture into large bowl. Add yeast mixture and egg; mix well. Add 2¹/₂ cups of the flour, ¹/₂ cup at a time, mixing well after each addition. Work in remaining ¹/₄ cup flour if needed to make a soft dough. Turn out onto lightly floured surface and knead about 2 minutes.

Cover dough with a towel and let rest about 5 minutes, for dough to firm up. (At this point, you can wrap dough in plastic wrap and refrigerate it until the next day. When ready to use, remove plastic wrap and place dough on lightly floured surface. Let dough stand at room temperature 15 minutes before proceeding with recipe.)

Add ¹/₂ cup softened butter to dough; incorporate it by hand. (You just squish the butter around until it can be kneaded.) Knead 2 or 3 minutes. The dough will be soft and sticky. Let dough rest 5 minutes while you get the sausage out of the refrigerator and lightly grease two baking sheets.

On floured board or countertop, roll out dough into a 24x15-inch rectangle. Crumble sausage and spread it evenly on top of dough. Starting with long side, carefully roll up dough and sausage, like a jelly roll. Using a sharp knife, cut roll into slices, 1 inch thick. Place slices about 2 inches apart on greased baking sheets. Cover and let rise 30 minutes.

Bake in a preheated 350-degree oven 20 to 25 minutes, or until sausage is browned and bread is golden brown.

Note: *By using a garlic or Italian sausage, you can change these break-fast roll-ups into hot appetizers. Resist the temptation to turn them into mini-pizzas by adding sauce and cheese, because that will overpower the delicate texture of the pastry crust.*

Sausage Roll-Ups

Yield: 18 rolls.

1 cup **whole milk**	3 cups **HODGSON MILL Naturally White Flour**
¼ cup **water**	
1 **egg**	2¼ teaspoons **FLEISCHMANN'S Bread Machine Yeast**
½ cup plus 2 tablespoons **butter**, at room temperature	
	1 (16-ounce) package **break-fast sausage**, uncooked
1 teaspoon **salt**	

Add milk, water, egg, butter, salt, flour and yeast to bread machine pan in the order suggested by manufacturer. Select **dough/manual cycle**.

When cycle is complete, remove dough from machine to a lightly floured surface. If necessary, knead in enough additional flour to make dough easy to handle. Roll dough to an 18x15-inch rectangle. Crumble sausage and spread over dough. Beginning at long side, roll up tightly as for a jelly roll. Pinch seam to seal. With a sharp knife, cut into 1-inch slices. Place slices on 2 lightly greased baking sheets. Cover and let rise in a warm, draft-free place about 30 minutes, or until doubled in size.

Bake in a preheated 350-degree oven 20 to 25 minutes, or until sausage is browned and bread is golden.

BUTTER PECAN BREAKFAST BREAD

Yield: 2 loaves.

Bread Break

I created this recipe when I was experimenting with some Amish Friendship Bread starter. The buttermilk is a quick substitute for the starter, which takes more than a week to develop fully.

This bread is best served slightly warm. Remember that bread continues to bake even after it comes out of the oven, so don't cut it while it's hot or the center may still be doughy. The miniloaf size is perfect for breakfast in bed or an afternoon snack over coffee with a friend.

³/₄ cup **buttermilk,** warmed in a saucepan

3 **eggs,** beaten

1 cup **vegetable oil**

2 teaspoons **vanilla extract**

1 cup **granulated sugar**

2 cups **HODGSON MILL Naturally White Flour**

1 (3.4-ounce) package **instant butterscotch pudding** mix

1 ¹/₂ teaspoons **baking powder**

¹/₄ teaspoon **baking soda**

1 cup chopped **pecans**

CINNAMON SUGAR:
¹/₂ cup **granulated sugar**

1 tablespoon **ground cinnamon**

Preheat oven to 350 degrees.

Combine buttermilk, eggs, oil, vanilla and sugar in a large mixing bowl; mix well.

Sift flour, dry pudding mix, baking powder and baking soda into bowl containing buttermilk mixture. (If you don't have a sifter, place dry ingredients in a separate bowl and stir with a fork until well blended, then add to buttermilk mixture.) Beat until well blended. Fold in pecans.

Grease two 9x5x3-inch loaf pans with shortening, then coat with cinnamon sugar (save the excess). Divide batter between the two pans. Sprinkle remaining cinnamon sugar on the top of the batter. Place immediately in preheated 350-degree oven and bake 50 to 55 minutes, or until a cake tester inserted in the center of the loaf comes out clean. Remove from pans and let cool on wire racks.

Note: If preferred, divide batter among five miniloaf pans. Reduce baking time to 40 to 45 minutes.

Tip: If you don't have a cake tester, use a single piece of uncooked spaghetti, which is both sturdy and long enough to use on a large loaf.

Shortcake

Yield: 6 servings.

2 cups **HODGSON MILL Naturally White Flour**

1 tablespoon **granulated sugar**

2 teaspoons **baking powder**

½ teaspoon **salt**

⅓ cup **solid vegetable shortening**

1 **egg**, well beaten

½ cup **milk**

Melted **butter**

Sift flour, sugar, baking powder and salt into a medium bowl; stir until well blended. Using a pastry blender or two knives, cut shortening into flour mixture until the mixture resembles coarse crumbs. Combine egg and milk in small bowl; mix well. Add to flour mixture. Stir until just moistened.

Turn out dough onto a floured surface. Knead 8 or 10 strokes. Divide dough into two equal pieces. Pat each piece into a 7½-inch round. Place one round in a greased 8-inch cake pan. Brush top of dough with melted butter. Place second round on top.

Bake in a preheated 450-degree oven 15 to 20 minutes, or until lightly browned. Remove from pan and let cool on a rack.

Serve shortcake split and filled with strawberries or other fruit of choice. Top with whipped cream or ice cream, if desired.

Note: If it's a hot day, refrigerate the shortening for about 15 minutes before use, or it will blend with the flour too much. The lightness of the shortcake depends upon the shortening and the dry ingredients being distinct.

If you go to the trouble to make your own shortcake, use your food processor or mixer to whip real whipped cream to use as a topping.

Bread Break

The Tremont Turkey Festival is one of my favorite Illinois celebrations. In addition to the hundreds of turkeys that are roasted and served, strawberry shortcake is a festival favorite. I learned that the festival organizers arrange with local church groups to make the shortcake in large batches, using quick biscuit mix, oil, sugar and water. I offer my mother's shortcake recipe instead. Because she's an experienced baker, her directions were much more abbreviated. For the sake of novices, I've expanded them somewhat.

I've never quite understood how shortcake got its name, because shortcake looks like bread to me, while shortbread looks like cookies. Some shortcake recipes call for more sugar, but I prefer for the sweetness to come from the fruit that is used. More sugar will make the dough brown too quickly in such a hot oven.

Apricot Skillet Bread

Yield: 1 (10-inch) flat bread; 8 servings.

Bread Break

My buddy Greg is concerned about eating healthfully, so one night I invited him over to develop a new flat bread recipe. This Apricot Skillet Bread was the result. Notice that there is no oil or butter in the batter, and it's relatively low in salt and sugar. The apricots are best fresh, but we had only canned the first time we made it and it turned out just fine. We also used low-fat peach yogurt, but feel free to experiment with other flavors and fruits.

The flavors of this bread are quite subtle, so try it warm by itself before adding toppings. We discovered that a light hand with the butter knife and just a small drizzle of honey accented the taste without overwhelming it.

I like this bread as a late-morning snack, accompanied by a delicate tea such as Formosa Oolong or Darjeeling.

1 cup **yogurt** (plain or flavored)

$^{1}/_{2}$ cup chopped **fresh** or **canned apricots**

2 **eggs** (or egg substitute)

1 cup **HODGSON MILL Organic Spelt Flour** or **Naturally White Flour**

$^{1}/_{2}$ cup **HODGSON MILL Yellow Corn Meal**

2 tablespoons **brown sugar**

1 tablespoon **HODGSON MILL Wheat Germ**

2 teaspoons **baking powder**

1 teaspoon **ground coriander**

$^{1}/_{2}$ teaspoon **ground ginger**

$^{1}/_{2}$ teaspoon **salt**

Preheat oven to 400 degrees. Lightly grease a 10-inch cast-iron skillet; place in the preheating oven for 5 minutes.

Warm yogurt in a medium saucepan over low heat until liquid. Remove from heat. Add apricots and eggs; stir until blended.

Combine spelt flour, cornmeal, brown sugar, wheat germ, baking powder, coriander, ginger and salt in a large bowl; stir until thoroughly mixed. Pour yogurt mixture over flour mixture; stir until just moistened.

Remove skillet from oven. Pour batter into heated skillet, smoothing the top of the batter with a spatula or spoon. Immediately return skillet to oven and bake 20 minutes. To test for doneness, insert toothpick in the center of the bread and remove; if it comes out clean, the bread is done. If not, return bread to oven for 5 minutes.

Leave bread in the skillet for 5 minutes after it comes out of the oven. Then remove the bread by placing one hand (protected by an oven mitt or towel) on top of the bread and turning the pan upside down with the other hand, catching the bread in your hand as it comes out. Let bread cool on a wire rack for 10 minutes, then cut into wedges and serve.

Note: Spelt, a grain cultivated since antiquity, is more easily digestible than wheat flour. I like the slightly sweet, nutty character it adds to bread. Spelt flour might not be readily available in your area, so feel free to substitute all-purpose flour. Be sure to use yellow cornmeal rather than a finely ground corn flour—you'll appreciate the added crunch. Father Marion's comment upon sampling this bread: "You can taste the texture."

FUNNEL CAKES

Yield: 4 funnel cakes.

3 **eggs**	2 teaspoons **baking powder**
1 1/4 cups **milk**	1/2 teaspoon **salt**
1 teaspoon **vanilla extract**	**Vegetable oil**, for frying
2 1/2 cups **HODGSON MILL Naturally White Flour**	**Confectioners' sugar** or **cinnamon sugar**, for topping (optional)
1/2 cup **granulated sugar**	

Combine eggs, milk and vanilla in a large bowl; beat until well blended. Put flour, sugar, baking powder and salt in a sifter; sift into bowl containing egg mixture. Stir to mix. Depending on the weather, you might need to add more flour or more milk. The batter should be about the same consistency as waffle batter.

Add oil to a depth of 1 1/2 inches in a deep, 12-inch skillet. Place over medium heat until oil reaches 350 degrees. Carefully pour batter into hot oil through a large funnel in a swirling or crisscross motion to form the funnel cake. Fry until golden brown and crispy. Turn once. Drain on paper towels. Repeat until all batter is used.

Serve funnel cakes topped with confectioners' sugar and/or cinnamon sugar (1/4 cup granulated sugar, 1 1/2 teaspoons cinnamon). You might want to place a dollop of ice cream on top, or use fruit toppings.

❧

Note: Mix the batter in a pitcher so it will be easy to pour. Experiment with the size of funnel you use, depending on whether you want a thin, crispy cake or a thicker, more doughy one. You might have to add more milk if your funnel has a small hole.

Bread Break

I spent a pleasant evening with a couple of alums trying to fine-tune this recipe. We did throw a lot of ruined batter away, but eventually we got what looked and tasted like a funnel cake from a county fair. One of our innovations was to cut the bottom out of a 9-inch disposable aluminum cake pan, and use the remaining ring as a form to keep the batter from spreading out all over the skillet. Carefully place the ring in the oil and remove it with tongs once the funnel cake has firmed up.

Yield: 2 loaves.

Bread Break

This is another of Mom's favorite recipes. It has won a ribbon no fewer than 21 times at the Heart of Illinois Fair. I can't guarantee you a blue ribbon, but you'll be a winner with your family and friends if you bake this raisin bread. The sugar topping forms a beautiful brown crust, and the milk makes for a soft, tender crumb.

2 packages **FLEISCHMANN'S Active Dry Yeast**

¼ cup warm **water**

1½ cups **milk**

3 tablespoons **butter**

2 tablespoons **granulated sugar**

2 teaspoons **salt**

2 **eggs**, beaten

5½ to 6 cups **HODGSON MILL Best for Bread Flour**, divided

1½ cups **raisins**

Melted **butter** and **granulated sugar**, for topping

Sprinkle yeast over warm water in a small bowl; stir to mix. Let stand 5 to 10 minutes, or until foamy.

Combine milk and butter in a small saucepan; heat until butter is nearly melted. Pour into a large mixing bowl and let cool to lukewarm. Add yeast mixture, sugar, salt and eggs; stir until blended. Add 5 cups of the flour, one cup at a time, stirring after each addition; mix until the dough is workable and pulls away from the side of the bowl. Add raisins; mix in by hand.

Turn out dough onto a lightly floured surface. Knead 5 minutes, adding enough of the remaining flour to make a smooth, elastic dough. Place dough in large oiled bowl; turn to coat. Cover with a clean towel and let rise in a warm, draft-free place about one hour, or until doubled in bulk.

Punch down dough. Knead briefly to work out larger air bubbles. Form dough into 2 loaves. Place in 2 greased 9x5x3-inch loaf pans. Cover; let rise 45 minutes, or until nearly doubled. Brush the top of each loaf with melted butter and sprinkle with sugar.

About 15 minutes before end of rising time, preheat oven to 425 degrees. Bake loaves for 10 minutes. Loosely cover loaves with aluminum foil and reduce oven temperature to 350 degrees. Bake 25 to 30 minutes, or until loaves sound hollow when tapped on the bottom. Remove from pans and let cool on wire racks.

RAISIN BREAD

Bread Machine

Yield: 1 (1 1/2-pound) loaf.

1/2 cup **milk**

1/4 cup plus 2 tablespoons **water**

2 tablespoons **butter** or **margarine**

1 **egg**

1 teaspoon **salt**

2 1/2 cups **HODGSON MILL Best for Bread Flour**

2 tablespoons **granulated sugar**, divided

1 1/2 teaspoons **FLEISCHMANN'S Bread Machine Yeast**

3/4 cup **raisins**

Add milk, water, butter, egg, salt, flour, 1 tablespoon of the sugar, yeast and raisins to bread machine pan in the order suggested by manufacturer. Select **basic cycle; medium/normal color setting**. During the final rise, sprinkle the remaining 1 tablespoon sugar on top of dough.

CINNAMON SWIRL BREAD

Yield: 2 loaves.

Bread Break

Cinnamon bread is the ultimate in comfort food, the quintessential mid-morning, after-school or midnight snack. Toasting is almost sine qua non in my opinion, unless the bread is sliced 15 minutes after it comes out of the oven. The nutmeg and cinnamon make the flavor suggestive of eggnog or custard. Those who like a stronger cinnamon flavor may consider doubling the amount of cinnamon used in the filling.

DOUGH:

1 cup **milk**

1 cup **sour cream**

3 tablespoons solid **vegetable shortening** or **butter**

5 1/2 to 6 cups **HODGSON MILL Best for Bread Flour** or **Naturally White Flour**, divided

1/4 cup **granulated sugar**

2 packages **FLEISCHMANN'S Active Dry Yeast**

2 teaspoons **salt**

1 tablespoon **vanilla extract**

3 **eggs**, beaten

FILLING:

2 tablespoons **butter**, softened

1/4 cup **granulated sugar**

1 tablespoon **ground cinnamon**

Pinch **ground nutmeg**

Combine milk, sour cream and shortening in a saucepan over low heat; stir occasionally until sour cream and shortening are melted and mixed in. Remove from heat. Let cool to lukewarm.

Combine 2 cups of the flour, sugar, yeast and salt in a large bowl; mix well. Blend milk mixture, vanilla and eggs into flour mixture; beat about 3 minutes. Add enough of the remaining flour to make a soft dough that pulls away from the side of the bowl.

Turn dough out onto a lightly floured surface. Knead 5 minutes, adding flour as needed to make a smooth and elastic dough. Lightly grease the surface of the dough; place dough in a greased bowl. Cover and let rise in a warm, draft-free place about 1 to 1 1/2 hours, or until doubled in bulk.

Punch down dough. Knead 2 minutes to work out the air bubbles. Divide dough into 2 equal pieces. On a lightly floured surface or pastry cloth, roll each piece of dough into a rectangle about 14 by 7 inches. Spread softened butter on dough, leaving a 1/2-inch border around the edge. Combine sugar, cinnamon and nutmeg; sprinkle over butter. Starting with the short edge, tightly roll up dough; seal the edges. Place in greased 9x5x3-

inch loaf pans. Cover with a clean towel and let rise 45 to 60 minutes, or until nearly doubled.

About 15 minutes before end of rising time, preheat oven to 375 degrees. Bake bread 40 to 45 minutes, or until top is golden and bread sounds hollow when tapped.

Remove from pans and let cool on a wire rack. If desired, while loaves are still hot, brush the tops with additional butter and sprinkle with additional cinnamon sugar.

Note: Be careful not to add too much flour, either in mixing or knead-ing, or the dough will be too stiff to roll out. It's better for the dough to be a bit too soft than too stiff. When sealing the edges of the loaf, brush the edge of the dough with a little milk if you have trouble getting it to stick.

I like to make this recipe in circular glass tube pans. Corning used to produce them, but I'm not sure if they're still available. I got mine at a rummage sale. They make a perfectly round slice of bread with a spiral of cinnamon in the center.

CINNAMON SWIRL BREAD

Yield: 1 (1 1/2-pound) loaf.

1/2 cup **milk**

1/2 cup **sour cream**

1 **egg**

1 1/2 tablespoons **butter**

1 1/2 teaspoons **vanilla extract**

1 teaspoon **salt**

2 1/2 cups **HODGSON MILL Best for Bread Flour**

2 tablespoons **granulated sugar**

1 1/2 teaspoons **FLEISCHMANN'S Bread Machine Yeast**

CINNAMON FILLING:

2 tablespoons **granulated sugar**

1 tablespoon **ground cinnamon**

1/4 teaspoon **ground nutmeg**

1 tablespoon **butter**, softened

Add milk, sour cream, egg, butter, vanilla, salt, flour, sugar and yeast to bread machine pan in the order suggested by manufacturer. Select **dough/manual cycle**.

While dough is mixing, prepare cinnamon filling. Combine sugar, cinnamon and nutmeg in small bowl; stir to blend. Set butter out to soften.

When cycle is complete, remove dough from machine to a lightly floured surface. If necessary, knead in enough additional flour to make dough easy to handle. Roll dough into a 14x7-inch rectangle. Spread softened butter on dough; sprinkle cinnamon filling on top. Beginning from the short end of the dough, roll up tightly as for a jelly roll. Pinch seam and ends to seal. Place, seam-side down, in greased 9x5-inch loaf pan. Cover; let rise in warm, draft-free place about 1 hour, or until doubled in size.

Bake in a preheated 375-degree oven 25 to 30 minutes, or until done. Remove from pan; let cool on wire rack.

If desired, brush top of loaf with additional butter while hot; sprinkle with additional cinnamon and sugar.

VEGGIE BREADS

CHOP BLOCK BREAD

Yield: 1 large loaf or 2 medium loaves.

Bread Break

I developed this bread when I was in the school of theology at St. Meinrad Archabbey in southern Indiana. I had been elected to the Peace and Justice Committee, and we proposed simple Lenten meals for Fridays, with plain salad, soup and homemade bread. After our first attempt, the response was so positive that some people suggested that we should serve our menu the rest of the year, and what we normally got on Fridays should be the penance! The money saved by serving this simpler meal was donated to food programs for the needy.

1 recipe **Basic Whole Wheat Bread** (page 18)

1 cup grated **Cheddar cheese**

$^1/_2$ cup finely chopped **onion**

$^1/_2$ cup chopped **carrots**

$^1/_2$ cup coarsely chopped **broccoli**

$^1/_4$ cup chopped **celery**

2 tablespoons chopped **fresh lovage** (see note)

Prepare dough for Basic Whole Wheat Bread according to recipe; mix Cheddar cheese into dough. Cover and let rise in a warm, draft-free place about 1 hour, or until doubled in bulk.

Combine onion, carrots, broccoli, celery and lovage in a bowl; toss to mix well.

Punch down dough. Knead briefly to work out large air bubbles. Pat dough into a large oval. Place mixed vegetables on top of dough. Fold dough in half over vegetables. Knead gently to distribute the vegetables. At first, the dough will fall apart and be a bit awkward to handle, but be patient and don't push too hard. Eventually, the vegetables will become incorporated into the dough, but without losing their shape.

Grease a large baking sheet and sprinkle it with cornmeal. Flatten the dough into a large oval about 2 inches thick. (If preferred, form dough into two loaves.) Place on prepared baking sheet. Cover and let rise 30 to 45 minutes, or until nearly doubled in bulk.

About 15 minutes before end of rising time, preheat oven to 350 degrees. Bake bread 45 to 55 minutes, or until top crust is firm and loaf sounds hollow when tapped. Cover loaf lightly with aluminum foil if it begins to brown too quickly. Remove from pan and let cool on rack.

Note: You can use just about any kind of dough for Chop Block Bread. You can add the cheese when the mixture is at the batter stage, or you can toss it with the vegetables just before they are kneaded in. You can try other kinds of cheese; I recommend Romano. You might want to substitute cauliflower or olives for one of the other vegetables.

Lovage is a plant with dark green, celery-like leaves. The flavor is that of a very strong celery. The seeds are commonly called celery seeds. If lovage is not available, substitute 1 teaspoon celery seeds.

Don't skimp on the flour. The vegetables add a lot of moisture, and a dough that is too soft will result in a soggy loaf.

The cheese in the bread can make it brown quickly, so keep an eye on these loaves during the first 20 or 30 minutes of baking.

Chop Block Bread

Bread Machine

Yield: 1 (1 ½-pound) loaf.

1 cup **water**

¼ cup chopped **carrot**

¼ cup chopped **broccoli**

2 tablespoons chopped **celery**

2 tablespoons **vegetable oil**

1 ½ tablespoons **brown sugar**

1 ½ teaspoons **salt**

1 tablespoon chopped **fresh lovage** (or ½ teaspoon **celery seeds**)

½ cup grated **Cheddar cheese**

1 ½ cups **HODGSON MILL Best for Bread Flour**

1 ½ cups **HODGSON MILL Whole Wheat Graham Flour**

1 ½ teaspoons **HODGSON MILL Vital Wheat Gluten**

2 teaspoons **FLEISCHMANN'S Bread Machine Yeast**

Add ingredients to bread machine pan in order suggested by the manufacturer, adding vegetables with water. Select **dough/manual cycle**.

When cycle is complete, remove dough from machine to lightly floured surface. Flatten the dough into a large oval about 2 inches thick. Place on greased baking sheet that has been sprinkled with cornmeal. Cover; let rise in a warm, draft-free place about 30 minutes, or until doubled in size.

Bake in a preheated 350-degree oven 45 minutes, or until done. Shield loaves with aluminum foil to prevent excess browning, if necessary. Remove from baking sheet; let cool on wire rack.

Pesto Spirals

I grow a lot of basil for the brethren, but it was only recently that I started making pesto, which is as good tossed with pasta as it is in these rolls. The basil, parsley and garlic absolutely have to be fresh for pesto to fulfill its culinary destiny.

Not long ago, I made a batch of these rolls for some friends of mine who have a toddler named Jack. He liked them so much that now whenever I call, he asks, "Fa Dom make biscuits?"

1 recipe **Basic White Bread** (page 14)

2 cups coarsely chopped **fresh basil leaves**

$\frac{1}{2}$ cup coarsely chopped **fresh parsley**

$\frac{1}{4}$ cup **pine nuts** or chopped **almonds**

4 cloves **garlic**

$\frac{1}{2}$ cup **olive oil**

$\frac{1}{2}$ teaspoon **salt**, or to taste

$\frac{1}{2}$ cup grated **Parmesan cheese**

1 **egg**, beaten (optional)

Prepare dough for Basic White Bread through the first rise.

While dough is rising, prepare pesto (or use one 8-ounce store-bought jar). To make your own pesto, combine basil, parsley, pine nuts, garlic, oil and salt in container of electric blender or food processor. Blend or process on high speed until you have a smooth purée; the nuts should be completely ground. Transfer mixture to a small bowl. Stir in Parmesan cheese. Taste and add more salt, if needed. Makes 1 cup.

Punch down dough. Knead lightly one minute. On a lightly floured surface, roll dough into a rectangle about 24 by 18 inches. Spread pesto on dough, leaving a 1-inch border. Starting from the long side, roll up jelly-roll style; pinch edges to seal. Brush the edges of the dough with some milk if you have trouble getting the dough to seal.

Grease a 14-inch pizza pan; dust it with cornmeal. Using a sharp knife, cut the roll of dough into 24, 1-inch-thick pieces. Place pieces, cut-side down, on prepared pan, arranging them in a spiral that starts in the center of the pan and works its way outward, slightly overlapping each piece onto the one next to it. Cover and let rise 30 to 45 minutes, or until nearly doubled.

About 15 minutes before end of rising time, preheat oven to 350 degrees. If desired, brush tops of rolls with beaten egg. Bake spiral 30 to 40 minutes, or until lightly browned and bread sounds hollow when tapped. Let cool slightly before serving. Place the pan in the center of the table and let people tear off pieces.

Note: *You can arrange and bake these rolls on two small pans, if necessary because of the size of your oven or your table. Sometimes I arrange the pieces in the shape of a flower, reserving a small ball of plain dough sprinkled with sesame seeds for the center.*

For the pesto, if you can't find (or can't afford) pine nuts, either almonds or walnuts can be substituted, but not peanuts. In extremis, you can omit the nuts entirely. You can substitute Romano or Asiago cheese for the Parmesan, but if you do, don't add salt until you've mixed in the cheese and tasted the pesto. Asiago in particular might have enough salt without adding more.

The moisture content of each of the cheeses will vary depending upon whether you get them fresh at the deli or buy the canister in the dairy section, so you may need to add more or less cheese to achieve the proper consistency. Pesto should be about the consistency of tomato paste, not a runny liquid. You may also add more basil leaves if you think the cheese is beginning to overwhelm the other flavors.

Pesto Spirals

Yield: 12 rolls.

1 recipe **Bread Machine Basic White Bread** (page 15)

1 cup coarsely chopped **fresh basil leaves**

¹/₄ cup coarsely chopped **fresh parsley**

¹/₄ cup **olive oil**

2 tablespoons **pine nuts** or chopped **almonds**

2 cloves **garlic**

¹/₄ teaspoon **salt**, or to taste

¹/₄ cup grated **Parmesan cheese**

Prepare dough using the **dough cycle**.

Place basil, parsley, oil, pine nuts, garlic and salt in container of electric blender. Cover and blend on high speed until smooth. Transfer mixture to a small bowl. Stir in Parmesan cheese. Taste; add more salt, if desired.

Grease a 12-inch pizza pan or baking sheet; sprinkle pan with cornmeal. Roll dough to 12x9-inch rectangle. Spread pesto on dough, leaving a 1-inch border. Beginning at long side, roll up tightly as for a jelly roll. Pinch seam to seal. With a sharp knife, cut roll into 12, 1-inch-thick pieces. Place pieces, cut-side down, on prepared pan, arranging them in a spiral that starts in the center of the pan and works its way outward. Overlap each piece slightly. Cover and let rise in a warm, draft-free place 30 to 45 minutes, or until doubled in size.

Bake in a preheated 350-degree oven 30 to 40 minutes, or until done. Remove from pan. Let cool slightly before serving.

ZUCCHINI CHEESE BATTER BREAD

Yield: 2 loaves.

2 cups **milk**

1 **egg**

2 tablespoons **vegetable oil**

2 tablespoons **granulated sugar**

2 packages **FLEISCHMANN'S Active Dry Yeast**

2 tablespoons **caraway seeds,** crushed

1 teaspoon **white pepper**

1 tablespoon **salt**

4 1/2 to 5 cups **HODGSON MILL Best for Bread Flour,** divided

1 1/2 cups shredded **baby Swiss cheese**

2 cups shredded **zucchini**

Combine milk, egg, oil, sugar and yeast in large mixing bowl. Stir until yeast is completely dissolved. Add caraway seeds, white pepper, salt and 2 cups of the flour. Beat well (about 150 strokes by hand or three minutes with an electric mixer). Stir in cheese and zucchini. Add 2 cups flour; beat well. Add enough of the remaining flour to make a thick batter that is still easy to manage. Stir until all flour is thoroughly incorporated. Use a rubber spatula to make sure there are no pockets of flour on the bottom of the bowl.

Cover with a clean towel and let rise in a warm, draft-free place about 1 hour. Thoroughly grease two 9x5x3-inch loaf pans. Stir batter down. Divide batter between pans. It should fill each pan halfway. Cover and let rise about 20 minutes, or until dough nearly reaches the top of the pan.

While dough is rising, preheat oven to 375 degrees. Bake about 45 minutes, or until a cake tester comes out clean and top crust feels solid. Let cool slightly in pans before attempting to remove loaves. Use a slender knife blade to loosen the sides of the loaf if it's stubborn.

❧

Note: This bread is best served warm on the day it's baked. Remember that breads containing cheese will tend to brown faster, so cover the top lightly with aluminum foil if you need to slow the browning process. The flavor of this bread is fairly subtle; you might want to add more caraway seeds, or perhaps substitute a stronger cheese.

Bread Break

Batter yeast breads are easy because you don't have to knead them, but that second rising of the loaves is a bit tricky. Don't let the batter over-rise or you'll have a major deflation as the bread cools, or there will be large holes at the top of each slice of bread. (This is the voice of experience talking. It happens to me all the time!) None of this will affect the flavor of the bread, which is superb, but it might make the appearance less than perfect.

I've used pans of all shapes and sizes for batter breads like this one: fluted metal tins, glass casseroles, stoneware bowls, miniloaf pans. Just make sure that whatever you use is oven-proof and safe for cooking. If you use glass, you might need to reduce the oven temperature by 25 degrees.

Yield: 2 loaves.

Bread Break

This bread was inspired by a huge crop of fresh spinach that Brother Luke brought in from our vegetable garden. I have served this bread at our monastery's meatless lunch on Friday. It's a delicious accompaniment to egg salad and French onion soup. If you don't like the flavor of feta cheese (or even if you do), try this recipe with Gruyere cheese. You might consider using a different dough, such as whole wheat.

1 recipe **Basic White Bread** (page 14)

1 cup coarsely chopped, blanched **fresh spinach** (see note)

$^1/_2$ cup chopped **walnuts**

8 ounces **feta cheese**, crumbled

Prepare dough for Basic White Bread through the first rise.

After dough has doubled, punch it down. Divide dough into two equal pieces. Roll out each piece on a lightly floured surface into a rectangle about 18 by 12 inches. On each rectangle of dough, spread $^1/_2$ cup spinach, $^1/_4$ cup walnuts and 4 ounces cheese. Starting at the wide end, tightly roll up dough, jelly-roll style. Pinch edges to seal. Brush a little water or milk on the edges if you have trouble getting dough to seal.

Place loaves, seam-side down, on a lightly greased baking sheet or in baguette pans. Cover and let rise about 45 minutes, or until nearly doubled. Using a razor blade or sharp knife, make several diagonal slashes in the top of each loaf, making sure to penetrate through the dough to expose the first layer of spinach and cheese.

About 15 minutes before end of rising time, preheat oven to 375 degrees. Bake 30 to 40 minutes, slightly longer if you prefer a crustier loaf, or until golden brown and loaves sound hollow when tapped.

Remove from pan and let cool on wire racks.

❦

Note: You'll need about 8 cups fresh spinach. Plunge spinach into boiling water for 1 minute; drain in a colander. Press spinach with paper towels to remove excess water. Coarsely chop with a sharp knife.

The reason you slash the tops of the loaves to expose the first layer is to allow steam to escape. Otherwise, the moisture in the spinach can cause a rapid expansion that will make the loaf split along one side. The escaping steam also promotes a marvelous crust.

Spinach Swirl

Bread Machine

Yield: 1 (1 ½-pound) loaf.

1 recipe **Bread Machine Basic White Bread** (page 15)

½ cup coarsely chopped, blanched **fresh spinach**

½ cup chopped **walnuts**, toasted

4 ounces **feta cheese**

Prepare dough using the **dough cycle**.

Roll dough to 18x12-inch rectangle. Spread spinach on dough; sprinkle with walnuts. Crumble feta cheese over top. Beginning at long side, roll up tightly as for a jelly roll. Pinch seam and ends to seal. Place loaf, seam-side down, on lightly greased baking sheet. Cover and let rise 35 to 45 minutes, or until doubled in size.

With a sharp knife or razor blade, make diagonal slashes across top of loaf. Bake in 375-degree oven 30 to 40 minutes, or until done. Remove from pan; let cool on wire rack.

Sourdough Breads

Bread Break

Sourdough bread is made with a sourdough starter, which contains yeast that has been allowed to ferment for a longer time than usual, thus creating the distinctive sour taste. The best method for getting sourdough starter is to obtain some from someone who uses it regularly. Some bakers have "mother" starters that are decades old. However, you also can use commercial yeast or try the old-fashioned method of capturing the wild yeast strains from the air. I have done both with excellent results.

The sourdough recipes that follow in this chapter were developed using sourdough starter made by the traditional method. Because the wild yeast strains can vary according to the ecosystem in which they thrive, your sourdough bread might taste somewhat different from other sourdough breads. Appreciate the uniqueness of whatever you create!

TRADITIONAL METHOD

2 cups **spring water** (non-chlorinated)

2 cups **HODGSON MILL Best for Bread Flour**

1 tablespoon **brown sugar** or **honey**

$^1/_2$ cup unseasoned, cooked **mashed potatoes** (optional)

Milk or **buttermilk** (optional)

Combine water, flour and brown sugar or honey in a non-reactive bowl. If desired, you can add mashed potatoes, or you can substitute milk or buttermilk for half of the water. Mix well. Cover bowl with open-weave cheesecloth and place outside on a warm, breezy day. The idea is to capture the wild yeast strains out of the air. Leave it out for several hours, or until the batter starts to develop bubbles and a pleasantly sour smell. Bring it inside and leave in a warm place for 2 or 3 days while the yeast develops. You might need to replenish the liquid each day; I often add more flour, as well.

There are no guarantees with this method. You might get sourdough, you might get mold, you might get wallpaper paste. But that's part of the adventure!

If after three days the batter smells unpleasant or seems a bit slimy, throw it out, sterilize the bowl and try again.

Once your starter is bubbling away, you can begin using it to make sourdough bread. You'll use 1 cup starter for your recipe. Replace that with an equal amount of flour and water. Place the replenished starter in a Mason jar or crock with a tight-fitting lid. Leave out for a couple of hours to develop, then close the lid and refrigerate for up to one week. The starter must be replenished once a week, so even if you don't use it to bake, take some out and feed the remainder with fresh liquid and flour. I alternate between flour and milk, sometimes using whole wheat flour or adding some mashed potatoes.

USING COMMERCIAL YEAST

Add 1 package FLEISCHMANN'S Active Dry Yeast to the ingredients given in the traditional method. Leave in a warm place, covered with plastic wrap, for several days while the sour flavor develops. Use and replenish as directed in traditional method. The starter will be sour, but not quite so wild tasting, and it will develop faster.

If you don't think you'll be baking sourdough at least once a week, you can use the starter entirely, and start from scratch with yeast each time.

Yield: 2 loaves.

Bread Break

Not every member of my community is fond of sour-dough bread, but I try to make it regularly for those who are. These basic baguettes are especially popular at lunch with homemade soup. I once gave a couple of loaves of this bread to the producer of our show to share with the production staff—but some-how the loaves never left his car and were "accidentally" taken straight home. So I've learned to make a larger batch so there are enough to share.

SPONGE:

1 cup **sourdough starter**

1 ½ cups warm **water**

2 tablespoons **granulated sugar**

3 cups **HODGSON MILL Best for Bread Flour**

DOUGH:

½ package **FLEISCHMANN'S Active Dry Yeast** (about 1 teaspoon)

¼ cup warm **water**

2 teaspoons **salt**

½ teaspoon **baking soda**

2 ½ to 3 ½ cups **HODGSON MILL Best for Bread Flour**, divided

For sponge: Combine starter, water, sugar and flour in a large, non-metal mixing bowl; mix well. Cover with a towel or plastic wrap and let stand at room temperature 24 to 48 hours. This is called the "sponge." The longer it develops, the stronger the sourdough flavor will be.

For dough: Sprinkle yeast over water in a small bowl; stir briefly. Let stand 5 to 10 minutes, or until foamy. Add yeast mixture, salt and baking soda to sponge; mix well. Add 1 cup of the flour; mix thoroughly. Add 1 cup flour and mix again. Turn out dough onto a lightly floured surface. Knead 6 to 8 minutes, adding enough of the remaining flour to make an elastic dough that is slightly sticky. Let dough rest 10 minutes.

Divide dough into 2 equal pieces. Roll each piece into a rectangle, 15 by 12 inches. Starting at the long side, roll up tightly; pinch seams to seal. Lightly roll the ends of each loaf to taper them. Place loaves on lightly greased cookie sheet or in lightly greased baguette pans. Cover and let rise about 45 minutes, or until doubled in bulk. Use a razor blade or sharp knife to make diagonal slashes in the top of each loaf.

While dough is rising, preheat oven to 375 degrees. For a firmer crust, place a pan of warm water on the bottom rack of the oven. Bake loaves 35 to 45 minutes, or until browned and breads sound hollow when tapped. Remove from pans and let cool on wire racks.

Note: *The use of bread flour in this recipe is fairly crucial. Bread flour is made from harder wheat, which can stand up to the long fermentation process. All-purpose flour will work, but the resulting loaves will not rise as well.*

You can use this dough to form sourdough bread bowls in which to serve soup. Form each half of the dough into a smooth ball, stretching the top and tucking the edges under to help prevent spreading during baking. Bake on a greased baking sheet, in oven-proof bowls or in fluted pans such as are used for brioche. After the bread has cooled, slice off the top and scoop out the soft inner part using a metal spoon or ice cream scoop, leaving about $1/2$ inch of bread and crust. Fill bread bowl with a cream soup, chowder or stew, and replace lid. Serve at once.

Bread Machine

SOURDOUGH BAGUETTES

Yield: 1 (1 ½-pound) loaf.

SPONGE:

½ cup **sourdough starter**

¾ cup warm **water**

1 tablespoon **granulated sugar**

1 ½ cups **HODGSON MILL Best for Bread Flour**

DOUGH:

¼ teaspoon **baking soda**

1 ¼ cups **HODGSON MILL Best for Bread Flour**

1 teaspoon **salt**

1 ¼ teaspoons **FLEISCHMANN'S Bread Machine Yeast**

For sponge: Combine sourdough starter, water, sugar and flour in a glass or ceramic bowl; stir well. Cover with plastic wrap and allow to ferment at room temperature 24 to 48 hours.

For dough: Add sponge, baking soda, flour, salt and yeast to bread machine pan in order suggested by the manufacturer, adding salt after the flour. (This will prevent the salt from coming in contact with the yeast in the sponge before the mixing begins.) Select **basic cycle; medium/normal crust.**

≈

Sourdough Whole Wheat Herb Bread

Yield: 2 large or 3 medium loaves.

Sponge:

1 cup **sourdough starter**

3 cups **HODGSON MILL Whole Wheat Graham Flour**

1 ½ cups warm **water**

3 tablespoons **honey**

½ teaspoon **ground nutmeg**

1 teaspoon **dried sage**

2 teaspoons **caraway seeds**, crushed

Dough:

1 package **FLEISCHMANN'S Active Dry Yeast**

¼ cup warm **water**

1 teaspoon **salt**

1 teaspoon **baking soda**

2 tablespoons **vegetable oil**, **butter** or **solid vegetable shortening**, softened

1 tablespoon **HODGSON MILL Vital Wheat Gluten** (optional)

4 to 5 ½ cups **HODGSON MILL Naturally White Flour**, divided

For sponge: Put starter in a large bowl. Add flour, water, honey, nutmeg, sage and caraway seeds. Mix well. Cover bowl with a cloth or plastic wrap and leave in a warm place for anywhere from 3 hours to 3 days. This is called the "sponge." The longer you let it develop, the stronger the distinctive sourdough flavor will be in your bread.

For dough: Sprinkle yeast over warm water in small bowl; stir to dissolve. Let stand 5 to 10 minutes, or until foamy.

When the sponge is ready, add yeast mixture, salt, baking soda, oil and gluten, mixing thoroughly. (The gluten is optional; it will make the loaf lighter and less dense.) Stir in 3 cups of the flour, one cup at a time, mixing well after each addition. Add enough of the remaining flour, ¼ cup at a time, to make a workable dough. Be careful not to add too much flour; sourdough is stickier than regular dough, and too much flour will yield a dry, crumbly loaf.

Turn out dough onto a floured surface. Knead 8 to 10 minutes,

Bread Break

This recipe uses a rather unusual combination of flavors, but it has never failed to please those who try it. If you don't care for the taste of caraway, omit it or substitute celery seeds.

I usually make the sponge after supper and leave it until the next day before forming the dough. You can even make the sponge the evening before, form the dough the next day before you go to work, and let the dough rise in the refrigerator. When you get home from work, take the dough out, punch it down and knead it for about two minutes. Then form your loaves and allow them to rise as usual. You might have to serve supper a little later than usual, but it will be worth the wait!

adding flour as needed to make a smooth dough that springs back into shape when pushed. Lightly oil the surface of the dough. Place in bowl, cover with a cloth and let rise in warm, draft-free place about 1 hour, or until doubled in bulk. Shape dough into loaves; you can either make loaves to put in greased loaf pans or make them free form on greased baking sheets. Cover and let rise about 1 hour, or until almost doubled.

While dough is rising, preheat oven to 375 degrees. Bake loaves about 1 hour, or until golden brown. If the tops start to brown too quickly (this can happen in breads made with honey), cover lightly with aluminum foil until the last 10 minutes of baking. Remove from pans and let cool on racks.

Sourdough Whole Wheat Herb Bread

Bread Machine

Yield: 1 (2-pound) loaf.

SPONGE:

$^1\!/_2$ cup **sourdough starter**

$^3\!/_4$ cup **water**

$1\,^1\!/_2$ cups **HODGSON MILL Whole Wheat Graham Flour**

$1\,^1\!/_2$ tablespoons **honey**

1 teaspoon **caraway seeds**, crushed

$^1\!/_2$ teaspoon **dried sage**

$^1\!/_4$ teaspoon **ground nutmeg**

DOUGH:

$^1\!/_4$ cup **water**

1 tablespoon **vegetable oil**

$^1\!/_2$ teaspoon **baking soda**

2 cups **HODGSON MILL Best for Bread Flour**

1 teaspoon **salt**

$1\,^1\!/_2$ teaspoons **HODGSON MILL Vital Wheat Gluten**

2 teaspoons **FLEISCHMANN'S Bread Machine Yeast**

For sponge: Combine sourdough starter, water, flour, honey, caraway seeds, sage and nutmeg in a glass or ceramic bowl; stir well. Cover with plastic wrap and let ferment for anywhere from 3 hours to 3 days.

For dough: Add sponge, water, oil, baking soda, flour, salt, gluten and yeast to bread machine pan in order suggested by the manufacturer, adding salt after the flour. (This will prevent the salt from coming in contact with the yeast in the starter before mixing begins.) Select **whole wheat/whole grain cycle; medium/normal color setting**.

Sourdough Onion Rye Bread

Yield: 3 round loaves.

Bread Break

Although fresh ingredients are usually preferable, every once in awhile a seasoning adds a unique flavor to bread. In this case, the onion powder is not the same as minced fresh onion, but the result is delicious; many people seem to prefer it. The loaves certainly disappeared quickly the first time I made them for the community. Our Father John of happy memory was especially fond of this bread and always managed to show up just as the loaves were cool enough to be cut and sampled!

Sponge:

1 cup **sourdough starter**

1 cup **HODGSON MILL Best for Bread Flour**

$^{1}/_{2}$ cup warm **water**

Dough:

1 package **FLEISCHMANN'S Active Dry Yeast**

$^{1}/_{4}$ cup warm **water**

1 cup unseasoned, cooked **mashed potatoes**

1 cup lukewarm **milk**

3 tablespoons **caraway seeds**

2 tablespoons **onion powder**

1 tablespoon **salt**

1 teaspoon **baking soda**

2 tablespoons **dark corn syrup**

4 cups **HODGSON MILL Rye Flour**, divided

3 to 4 cups **HODGSON MILL Best for Bread Flour**, divided

For sponge: Put starter in a large glass or ceramic bowl. Add flour and water; mix well. Cover with plastic wrap and let ferment 4 to 12 hours. This is called the "sponge." The longer it develops, the stronger the sourdough flavor will be.

For dough: Sprinkle yeast over warm water in small bowl; stir to dissolve. Let stand 5 to 10 minutes, or until foamy.

When the sponge is ready to use, combine mashed potatoes, milk, caraway seeds, onion powder, salt, baking soda and corn syrup in a large bowl; mix well. Add sponge and yeast mixture; mix well.

Add 2 cups of the rye flour; beat for about 100 strokes. Add remaining rye flour, 1 cup at a time, mixing well after each addition. Add 2 cups of the bread flour, 1 cup at a time, mixing well after each addition. Let dough rest about 10 minutes while the flour absorbs the liquid. Add enough of the remaining bread flour to make a workable dough. Turn out dough onto lightly floured surface. Knead 10 to 12 minutes. The dough should be smooth but rather sticky, and will not be as elastic or "lively" as white bread dough. Lightly coat dough with butter and put it in the rinsed mixing bowl. Cover and let rise in a warm, draft-free place 1 to 1 1/2 hours, or until doubled in bulk.

Punch down dough. Turn out onto lightly floured surface. Knead about 3 minutes to work out the larger air bubbles. Form dough into three round loaves. Lightly grease loaves; place on greased baking sheets. Cover and let rise about 1 hour, or until almost doubled. The loaves might spread out more than they rise, but don't worry; they'll gain a bit more height during the first 10 minutes of baking. This is called "oven spring." Use a sharp knife to cut four crisscross slashes in the top of each loaf.

While dough is rising, preheat oven to 375 degrees. Bake loaves 40 to 50 minutes, or until loaves make a hollow thump when tapped on the bottom. Remove from pans and let cool on racks.

 **Bread Machine**

Sourdough Onion Rye Bread

Yield: 1 (1 ¹/₂-pound) loaf.

SPONGE:

¹/₃ cup **sourdough starter**

3 tablespoons warm **water**

¹/₃ cup **HODGSON MILL Best for Bread Flour**

DOUGH:

¹/₂ cup **milk**

¹/₃ cup unseasoned, cooked **mashed potatoes**

1 tablespoon **caraway seeds**

2 teaspoons **onion powder**

2 teaspoons **dark corn syrup**

¹/₄ teaspoon **baking soda**

2 cups **HODGSON MILL Best for Bread Flour**

1 teaspoon **salt**

²/₃ cup **HODGSON MILL Rye Flour**

1 ¹/₂ teaspoons **FLEISCHMANN'S Bread Machine Yeast**

For sponge: Combine sourdough starter, water and flour in a glass or ceramic bowl; stir well. Cover with plastic wrap and allow to ferment 4 to 12 hours.

For dough: Add sponge, milk, mashed potatoes, caraway seeds, onion powder, corn syrup, baking soda, bread flour, salt, rye flour and yeast to bread machine pan in order suggested by the manufacturer, adding salt after the bread flour. (This will prevent the salt from coming in contact with the yeast in the sponge before mixing begins.) Select **whole wheat/whole grain cycle; medium/normal color setting**.

Sourdough Pumpernickel Bread

Yield: 3 round loaves.

SPONGE:

1 cup **sourdough starter**

1 cup warm **water**

1 cup **HODGSON MILL Best for Bread Flour**

DOUGH:

1 package **FLEISCHMANN'S Active Dry Yeast**

1/4 cup warm **water**

1 cup unseasoned, cooked **mashed potatoes**

1 cup lukewarm **milk**

1/2 cup **molasses**

1/4 cup (1/2 stick) **butter**, softened

2 tablespoons **brown sugar**

1 tablespoon **salt**

1 teaspoon **baking soda**

1 cup **HODGSON MILL Yellow Corn Meal**

3 tablespoons **caraway seeds**

2 tablespoons **unsweetened cocoa powder**

2 tablespoons **HODGSON MILL Wheat Germ**

4 cups **HODGSON MILL Rye Flour or pumpernickel flour**, divided

3 to 4 cups **HODGSON MILL Best for Bread Flour**, divided

For sponge: Put starter in a large glass or ceramic bowl. Add water and flour; mix well. Cover with plastic wrap and let ferment 4 to 12 hours. This is called the "sponge." The longer it develops, the stronger the sourdough flavor will be.

For dough: Sprinkle yeast over warm water in small bowl; stir to dissolve. Let stand 5 to 10 minutes, or until foamy.

When the sponge is ready to use, combine yeast mixture, mashed potatoes, milk, molasses, butter, brown sugar, salt and baking soda in a large mixing bowl; mix well. Add the sponge, cornmeal, caraway seeds, cocoa powder and wheat germ; mix well.

Add 2 cups of the rye flour; beat for about 100 strokes. Add remaining rye flour, 1 cup at a time, mixing well after each addition. Add 2 cups of the bread flour, 1 cup at a time, mixing well after each addition. Let dough rest about 10 minutes while the

Bread Break

Pumpernickel was developed during a wheat shortage, when an enterprising baker added several different flours to make his white flour last longer. The resulting bread has remained popular ever since. This pumpernickel bread has a lighter color than the black pumpernickel you see in stores. If you use real pumpernickel flour, rather than regular rye flour, the resulting loaves will be more dense. Pumpernickel flour is coarsely ground and the particles tend to "cut" the gluten molecules so they don't trap the carbon dioxide produced by the sourdough yeast. You might want to try it both ways and see which you prefer.

cornmeal and wheat germ absorb the liquid. Add enough of the remaining bread flour to make a workable dough. Turn out dough onto lightly floured surface and knead 10 to 12 minutes. The dough should be smooth but rather sticky, and will not be as elastic or "lively" as white bread dough. Lightly coat dough with butter and put it in the rinsed mixing bowl. Cover and let rise in a warm, draft-free place 1 to 1 1/2 hours, or until doubled in bulk.

Punch down dough. Turn out onto lightly floured surface. Knead about 3 minutes to work out the larger air bubbles. Form dough into three round loaves. Lightly grease loaves; place on greased baking sheets. Cover and let rise about 1 hour, or until almost doubled. The loaves might spread out more than they rise, but don't worry; they'll gain a bit more height during the first 10 minutes of baking, This is called "oven spring." Use a sharp knife to cut four crisscross slashes in the top of each loaf.

While dough is rising, preheat oven to 375 degrees. Bake loaves 40 to 50 minutes, or until loaves make a hollow thump when tapped on the bottom. Remove from pans and let cool on racks.

Sourdough Pumpernickel Bread

Yield: 1 (1½-pound) loaf.

SPONGE:

⅓ cup **sourdough starter**

⅓ cup warm **water**

⅓ cup **HODGSON MILL Best for Bread Flour**

DOUGH:

½ cup **milk**

⅓ cup unseasoned, cooked **mashed potatoes**

2½ tablespoons **molasses**

1 tablespoon **butter**

1 tablespoon **caraway seeds**

2 teaspoons **brown sugar**

2 teaspoons **unsweetened cocoa powder**

¼ teaspoon **baking soda**

1½ cups **HODGSON MILL Best for Bread Flour**

1 teaspoon **salt**

¾ cup **HODGSON MILL Rye Flour**

⅓ cup **HODGSON MILL Yellow Corn Meal**

1 tablespoon **HODGSON MILL Vital Wheat Gluten**

2 teaspoons **HODGSON MILL Wheat Germ**

1½ teaspoons **FLEISCHMANN'S Bread Machine Yeast**

For sponge: Combine sourdough starter, water and flour in a glass or ceramic bowl; stir well. Cover with plastic wrap and allow to ferment 4 to 12 hours.

For dough: Add sponge, milk, mashed potatoes, molasses, butter, caraway seeds, brown sugar, cocoa powder, baking soda, bread flour, salt, rye flour, cornmeal, gluten, wheat germ and yeast to bread machine pan in order suggested by the manufacturer, adding salt after the bread flour. (This will prevent the salt from coming in contact with the yeast in the sponge before mixing begins.) Select **whole wheat/whole grain cycle; medium/normal crust setting.**

Ethnic Breads

Austrian Povitica

Yield: 1 loaf; 24 to 36 servings.

Bread Break

This recipe has been in my family for four generations. My great-grandmother, Frances Zunic Sardick, brought it to this country from Austria.

Povitica is a traditional holiday bread. In my family, it is a special treat for Easter, after Lenten fasts have ended and meals can be served with meat once again. When my mother was a little girl, her mother used to make it on Good Friday to serve on Saturday night. How she could stand to fry bacon and bake bread on the most important day of fast and abstinence in the church calendar, I can't imagine! She certainly was made of sterner stuff than Mom and Grandpa Frankie, who would leave the house and visit every church in a 25-mile radius to escape the tempting aromas.

You often see Croatian or Slovenian versions of this bread, usually called *potica*, which use ground walnuts, cream and a much sweeter

1 recipe **Basic White Bread** (page 14)

1 1/2 pounds **bacon**

2 tablespoons **granulated sugar**

6 **eggs**, thoroughly beaten

1 pound chopped **walnuts** (about 4 cups)

Prepare dough for Basic White Bread (or any simple white bread recipe) through the first rise. While dough is rising, chop the bacon into small pieces. Fry bacon until partly cooked, but not crisp. Drain on paper towels; set aside.

After dough has doubled, punch down dough. Knead 3 minutes to work out the air bubbles. Place dough on a large, floured cloth. Roll out dough to a 30x24-inch rectangle, about 1/2 inch thick. Spread bacon pieces evenly over dough. Sprinkle sugar over bacon. Carefully pour eggs over bacon-topped dough. Sprinkle walnuts over all.

Pulling up on the edge of the cloth to help get started, roll up the dough lengthwise, jelly-roll style. Pull slightly on the dough to get a tight roll, but be careful not to tear holes in the dough. Seal edges. Form the roll into a round loaf with the two ends tucked into the center. Place in a lightly greased 13x9x2-inch baking pan. Cover with a clean cloth and let rise in a warm, draft-free place about 50 minutes, or until doubled in bulk.

While loaf is rising, preheat oven to 450 degrees. If any of the egg mixture leaks out during rising, brush it over the top of the loaf for a glaze. (In any case, get as much of the egg out of the bottom of the pan as possible, or it will cause the bottom crust to burn.) Bake loaf for 10 minutes, then reduce oven temperature to 350 degrees and bake about 40 minutes, or until nicely browned. If your oven doesn't bake evenly, turn the loaf every 10 or 15 minutes to ensure the bread is being baked thoroughly on all sides. Serve warm.

Austrian Povitica

Yield: 1 loaf.

1 recipe **Bread Machine Basic White Bread** (page 15)

1/2 pound **bacon**, chopped and partly cooked

1 tablespoon **granulated sugar**

2 **eggs**, beaten

1 cup chopped **walnuts**

dough rolled into very thin layers. Potica is quite popular at Christmas in our area, but I find it too dry and a bit dull compared to this beauty, which bakes up as a large, dramatic loaf with exquisite flavors and textures.

Add ingredients of Basic White Bread in bread machine pan in the order suggested by manufacturer. Select **dough/manual cycle**.

When cycle is complete, remove dough from machine. Roll onto a large, floured cloth to 12x15-inch rectangle. Spread bacon bits evenly over dough; sprinkle sugar on top. Pour beaten eggs over bacon and dough. Sprinkle with walnuts. Beginning from long end of the dough, roll up tightly as for jelly roll. Pinch seam and ends to seal. Roll into a round loaf with the two edges tucked into the center. Place in lightly greased 13x9x2-inch baking pan. Cover; let rise in warm, draft-free place until doubled in size, about 1 hour.

Bake in a preheated 450-degree oven for 10 minutes; reduce heat to 350 degrees and continue baking for 30 minutes, or until done. If necessary, cover loaf with foil to prevent excessive browning. Remove from pan; let cool on wire rack.

SWEDISH LIMPA RYE BREAD

Yield: 2 round loaves.

I confess that I don't much care for rye bread, mainly because I don't like the flavor of caraway seeds, which most commercial bakeries seem to insist upon. But the subtle blend of coffee, orange and anise in this bread is a delightful surprise, like aromatherapy for your whole house!

There are dozens of variations on limpa rye, so feel free to experiment. Try adding a teaspoon of ground cumin or cardamom, a tablespoon of caraway seeds, or double the amount of anise. You can double the amount of orange peel, or try lemon peel instead. For a delicious breakfast bread that makes excellent toast, add one cup of raisins to the dough before the final cup of flour. Consider using a stout ale instead of the coffee.

If you use finely ground rye instead of the coarser stone-ground flour, you'll get a lighter loaf with a finer texture, but my monastery

$1/4$ cup **brown sugar**

2 packages **FLEISCHMANN'S Active Dry Yeast**

1 tablespoon **HODGSON MILL Vital Wheat Gluten** (optional)

3 cups **HODGSON MILL Rye Flour**, divided

2 cups lukewarm **coffee**

$1/4$ cup ($1/2$ stick) **butter**, melted

Grated **peel** of 1 medium **orange** (about 2 teaspoons)

Juice of 1 medium **orange** (about $1/4$ cup)

1 tablespoon **anise seeds**, crushed

2 teaspoons **salt**

$2 1/2$ to 3 cups **HODGSON MILL Best for Bread Flour**, divided

Combine brown sugar, yeast, gluten and 2 cups of the rye flour in a large mixing bowl; mix until thoroughly blended. Pour in coffee and butter; beat for about 200 strokes. Let dough rest 5 minutes as the yeast develops and the liquid is absorbed.

During this time, grate the peel of the orange, then juice the orange. Add peel and juice to dough. Add crushed anise seeds and salt. Stir until blended. Add remaining 1 cup rye flour; stir until incorporated.

At this point, abandon the spoon and add 2 cups of the bread flour by hand. Turn out dough onto a floured surface. Knead, adding at least $1/2$ cup bread flour, or more if the dough seems unmanageable. Remember: Rye flour dough will be stickier than white flour dough, so don't add too much flour at a time or you might end up with a dry, crumbly loaf. Knead for a total of 10 to 12 minutes, or until the dough is smooth and only slightly sticky.

Lightly butter the surface of the dough; place dough in rinsed mixing bowl. Cover with a clean towel and let rise in a warm, draft-free place about $1 1/2$ hours, or until doubled in bulk.

Punch down dough; knead 2 minutes to work out the larger air pockets and reactivate the yeast. Divide dough into two equal pieces. Form each piece into a round loaf. Place loaves side by side on a lightly greased baking sheet. Cover and let rise 45 to

60 minutes, or until nearly doubled. Use a razor blade or sharp knife to make 3 diagonal slashes in top of each loaf.

While dough is rising, preheat oven to 375 degrees. Bake loaves on middle shelf 40 to 45 minutes, or until crusty and well browned, and loaves sound hollow when tapped. They will be heavier and denser than white bread, so don't let that distress you. Remove from pan and let cool thoroughly on wire racks before storage.

Note: This bread will keep longer than other breads, and also freezes well. When grating the peel of citrus fruits, use just the thin, colored outer layer, which is called the zest. The white layer underneath is bitter.

brethren seem to prefer the heartier version. You also can use a higher proportion of white flour.

Limpa makes a great accompaniment to baked ham, or a thick ham and bean soup. Try it as a base for a Reuben sandwich, or just spread it with cream cheese.

SWEDISH LIMPA RYE BREAD

Yield: 1 (1 ½-pound) loaf.

1 cup brewed **coffee**

2 tablespoons **butter** or **margarine**

¼ cup **orange juice**

1 teaspoon **salt**

1 ½ cups **HODGSON MILL Best for Bread Flour**

1 ½ cups **HODGSON MILL Rye Flour**

2 tablespoons **brown sugar**

2 ¼ teaspoons **FLEISCHMANN'S Bread Machine Yeast**

1 teaspoon freshly grated **orange peel**

1 ½ teaspoons **anise seeds**

1 ½ teaspoons **HODGSON MILL Vital Wheat Gluten** (optional)

Add ingredients to bread machine pan in the order suggested by manufacturer. Select **dough/manual cycle**.

When cycle is complete, remove dough from machine to a lightly floured surface. If necessary, knead in enough additional flour to make dough easy to handle. Shape dough into a ball; place on greased baking sheet. Cover; let rise in warm, draft-free place about 45 minutes, or until doubled in size. Using a sharp knife, make 3 diagonal slashes on top of dough.

Bake in a preheated 375-degree oven 35 to 40 minutes, or until done. Remove from sheet; let cool on wire rack.

SYRIAN BREAD

Yield: 20 to 25 pocket breads.

Bread Break

Similar to Greek pita bread, this Syrian bread recipe came from my dear friend Stephanie, who of course got it from her mother. Stephanie says, "As far as the world's breads are concerned, I rank it right up there at the tippy top." It's especially fun to make these if you have a window in your oven and can watch them puff.

These breads are great for pocket sandwiches filled with everything from meat to cheese to vegetables. I especially recommend them for anyone who is dieting, because grilled vegetables with a little nonfat dressing make a great stuffing for these breads.

1 package **FLEISCHMANN'S Active Dry Yeast**

¼ cup warm **water**

11 cups **HODGSON MILL Naturally White Flour**

1 teaspoon **salt**

3 cups warm **water**

2 tablespoons **olive oil**

Sprinkle yeast over ¼ cup warm water in small bowl; stir briefly. Let stand 5 to 10 minutes, or until foamy.

Combine flour and salt in large mixing bowl; stir to mix. Make a well in the center of the flour mixture. Add yeast mixture, 3 cups warm water and oil. Using a wooden spoon, gradually draw the flour from the sides to mix with the liquid. When the dough begins to solidify, abandon the spoon and use your hands. Turn out dough onto a lightly floured surface. Knead about 10 minutes, or until elastic. Rub surface of dough with oil; place in rinsed mixing bowl. Cover and let rise in a warm, draft-free place about 1 ½ hours, or until doubled in volume.

Punch down dough. Knead lightly. Put a towel on a baking sheet or other surface; cover towel with plastic wrap. Form the dough into balls about the size of a small orange. Place dough balls on plastic wrap. Cover balls with another sheet of plastic wrap and top with another towel. Let rise about 1 hour.

Preheat oven to 500 degrees. Heat a baking stone or heavy metal baking sheet in oven. Roll balls into thin ovals and place on baking stone or baking sheet. Bake 4 to 5 minutes, or until dough puffs up. Remove from oven and stack on top of each other or side by side, so the air pocket will deflate. Cover breads with a towel while they cool, to help keep them soft.

⟨≫⟩

Note: *You'll notice the remarkably small proportion of salt in the recipe. That's because the flavor is supposed to come from the sandwich stuffings. You might want to experiment with adding more salt, but I wouldn't go above 2 teaspoons or the yeast will be seriously inhibited.*

Syrian Bread

Bread Machine

Yield: 10 pocket breads.

1 1/4 cups plus 1 tablespoon **water**

2 teaspoons **olive oil**

1 1/2 teaspoons **salt**

3 3/4 cups **HODGSON MILL Best for Bread Flour**

1 3/4 teaspoons **FLEISCHMANN'S Bread Machine Yeast**

Add ingredients to bread machine pan in order suggested by the manufacturer. Select **dough/manual cycle**.

When cycle is complete, remove dough from machine to a lightly floured surface. If necessary, knead in enough additional flour to make dough easy to handle. Divide dough into 10 equal pieces. Shape each piece into a smooth ball. Place a towel on a baking sheet or other surface; cover towel with plastic wrap. Place dough balls on plastic wrap. Cover balls with another sheet of plastic wrap and top with another towel. Let rest 30 minutes.

Place a baking stone or a heavy baking sheet on bottom rack of oven. Preheat oven to 500 degrees. Roll balls into thin ovals (about 1/8 inch thick). Bake 4 to 5 minutes, or until puffed and the top just begins to brown. Remove breads from oven and stack them on top of each other so the pockets deflate. Cover breads with a towel while they cool, to keep them soft.

TOMATO BASIL FOCACCIA

Yield: 2 flat breads.

Bread Break

One night I was making Papa Dom's Pizza Topping (page 100) with beefsteak tomatoes from our garden. They were slightly overripe, so I had to drain a lot of juice out of them. The juice was so fragrant and pulpy that I just had to use it for something, so I developed this focaccia recipe. One loaf went to the monks' refectory and one to the faculty lunch table; neither loaf survived the experience!

DOUGH:

2 cups **tomato juice**

$^1/_4$ cup chopped **sun-dried tomatoes**

1 package **FLEISCHMANN'S Active Dry Yeast**

1 cup **HODGSON MILL Whole Wheat Graham Flour**

2 tablespoons **olive oil**

$^1/_4$ cup finely chopped **fresh basil**

2 teaspoons **salt**

4 to 4$^1/_2$ cups **HODGSON MILL Best for Bread Flour**, divided

TOPPING:

Olive oil

1 cup coarsely chopped **fresh herbs** (chives, thyme, rosemary, etc.)

Kosher salt

Heat tomato juice in a saucepan over low heat until scalding (just below boiling); do not allow to boil. Add sun-dried tomatoes; let mixture cool to lukewarm. Transfer to a large mixing bowl. Stir in yeast and whole wheat flour. Let rest 10 minutes. Add olive oil, basil and salt; mix well, about 100 strokes by hand. Add bread flour, 1 cup at a time, mixing after each addition, until you get a soft dough that is rather sticky. Knead dough on a lightly floured surface 5 to 8 minutes, or until dough is smooth and elastic but still a bit sticky. (Be careful not to add too much flour while kneading.)

Lightly oil the surface of the dough. Place dough in rinsed mixing bowl. Cover with a clean towel and let rise in a warm, draft-free place 1 to 1$^1/_2$ hours, or until doubled in bulk. Punch down dough. Knead one minute. Cover dough and let rise in bowl about 45 minutes.

Punch down dough. Divide into 2 equal portions. Flatten each portion into a round, flat loaf, about $^3/_4$ inch thick. Place loaves on an ungreased baking sheet that has been sprinkled with cornmeal (you might need 2 sheets).

For topping, brush about 1 tablespoon olive oil on each loaf. Let rise, uncovered, about 30 minutes. Dimple the dough with your forefinger, spacing dimples about $1/2$ inch apart. Mix herbs with enough olive oil to coat thoroughly; spread herb mixture on loaves. Lightly sprinkle kosher salt on loaves.

Meanwhile, preheat oven to 400 degrees. Bake loaves about 20 minutes, or until lightly browned. Remove from oven and let loaves cool for 10 minutes before serving.

⁓

Note: *If you have a baking stone, preheat it in the oven. Use a peel to slide the loaves off the baking sheet and onto the stone. The resulting crust will be much better than if you use a baking sheet.*

If you don't have fresh herbs, use dried and reduce the amount by half, but put them on top of the bread as it comes out of the oven because dried herbs will burn under the intense heat of baking.

Canned tomato juice will work, but omit the salt, because commercial tomato juice is pretty salty. Also, the resulting tomato flavor might be quite strong and have a slight metallic tang to it.

This recipe can be halved, but it's so good, I doubt you'll have any leftovers. The second loaf will keep well in the freezer for about a month.

TOMATO BASIL FOCACCIA

Yield: 1 flat bread.

DOUGH:

1 cup **tomato juice**

2 tablespoons chopped **sun-dried tomatoes** (soaked in tomato juice for 5 minutes)

1 tablespoon **olive oil**

1 teaspoon **salt**

2 cups **HODGSON MILL Best for Bread Flour**

¹/₂ cup **HODGSON MILL Whole Wheat Graham Flour**

1 ¹/₂ teaspoons **FLEISCHMANN'S Bread Machine Yeast**

1 tablespoon finely chopped **fresh basil**

TOPPING:

2 tablespoons **olive oil**, divided

¹/₂ cup coarsely chopped **fresh herbs** (chives, rosemary, thyme, etc.)

¹/₂ teaspoon **kosher salt**

Add dough ingredients to bread machine pan in the order suggested by manufacturer. Select **dough/manual cycle**.

When cycle is complete, remove dough from machine to a lightly floured surface. If necessary, knead in enough additional flour to make dough easy to handle. Form dough into a ball; flatten ball to a 12-inch round. Place on ungreased baking sheet that has been sprinkled with cornmeal.

Brush 1 tablespoon olive oil on top of loaf. Let rise, uncovered, in warm, draft-free place about 30 minutes, or until almost doubled in size. Poke dough randomly with fingertips to form dimples. Mix herbs with remaining 1 tablespoon olive oil; spread over dough. Sprinkle kosher salt on top.

Bake in a preheated 400-degree oven 20 minutes, or until done. Serve warm.

Southwest Cornmeal Muffins

Yield: 12 muffins.

1 cup **milk**

1 **egg**, beaten

¼ cup **solid vegetable shortening**, melted (bacon fat can be substituted)

¼ cup minced **red onion**

1 tablespoon chopped **fresh cilantro**

¼ cup crisply cooked and crumbled **bacon**

2 tablespoons chopped **chili peppers**

1 cup **HODGSON MILL Yellow Corn Meal**

¾ cup **HODGSON MILL Naturally White Flour**

3 teaspoons **baking powder**

½ teaspoon **salt**

Preheat oven to 425 degrees.

Combine milk, egg and melted shortening in medium bowl; stir to mix. Add onion, cilantro, bacon and chiles; stir until blended. Place cornmeal, flour, baking powder and salt in a sifter; sift into the milk mixture. Stir until just blended.

Using a ¼-cup measure, drop batter into lightly greased muffin tins. Bake 15 to 20 minutes, or until tops of muffins are lightly browned. Cool slightly and serve warm.

Bread Break

I really don't care for the flavor of cilantro, but it's a staple of Southwest cooking, and those who enjoy eating Tex-Mex will love these muffins. They go great with Meatless Chili Soup (see page 106), so feel free to omit the bacon for a veggie version.

Yield: 2 flat breads.

Bread Break

The French word *fougasse* is related to the Italian word *focaccia*. Both come from the Latin word *focus*, meaning "hearth." Both breads were cooked on a flat stone placed on the embers of the fire. In Provence, you can find fougasse adorned with everything from cheese to bacon to anchovies, but this *pain aux olives* is a classic.

In addition to the ladder shape, fougasse also is made with pairs of diagonal slashes that form a "tree of life" shape (see illustrations). Both are designed to facilitate breaking off pieces of bread rather than slicing it. I myself prefer the ladder shape because it reminds me of the chapter of the *Rule of St. Benedict* that speaks of "the ladder of humility."

1 ½ cups warm **water**

1 package **FLEISCHMANN'S Active Dry Yeast**

1 cup **HODGSON MILL Whole Wheat Graham Flour**

½ cup **HODGSON MILL Buckwheat Flour**

2 teaspoons **salt**

1 tablespoon **olive oil**

¾ cup coarsely chopped pitted **ripe (black) olives**

3 cups **HODGSON MILL Best for Bread Flour**, divided

Additional pitted and sliced **ripe (black) olives**, for topping (optional)

Combine water, yeast, whole wheat flour, buckwheat flour, salt and oil in a large bowl. Beat for 100 strokes. Cover and let rest about 15 minutes, to allow the yeast to develop.

During this time you can pit and chop the olives. Be sure to drain them well on paper towels, or the proportion of liquid in the dough will be affected.

Add 2 cups of the bread flour to the yeast mixture; beat until thoroughly incorporated. Add olives; stir until evenly distributed. Add enough of the remaining bread flour to make a firm, slightly sticky dough. Turn out dough onto a lightly floured surface. Knead 12 to 15 minutes, adding more flour as needed to keep the dough manageable. When the dough is smooth and elastic, lightly oil the surface. Place dough in a bowl; cover and let rise in a warm, draft-free place about 1 hour, or until doubled in bulk.

Punch down dough. Knead it lightly to work out the larger air pockets. Divide dough into 2 equal pieces. On a lightly floured surface, roll each piece into an oval about ½ inch thick. Place each piece on a lightly greased baking sheet; use two baking sheets, if necessary. Using a sharp knife or razor blade, make four or five parallel slashes, starting about 1 inch from one edge and going across the bread to within 1 inch of the other edge. Pull the slashes apart slightly to enlarge the opening, to accentuate the "ladder" shape. If desired, decorate the tops with sliced olives. Cover with a clean towel and let rise 30 to 45 minutes until almost doubled.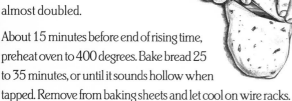

About 15 minutes before end of rising time, preheat oven to 400 degrees. Bake bread 25 to 35 minutes, or until it sounds hollow when 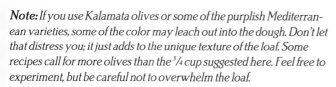 tapped. Remove from baking sheets and let cool on wire racks.

Note: *If you use Kalamata olives or some of the purplish Mediterranean varieties, some of the color may leach out into the dough. Don't let that distress you; it just adds to the unique texture of the loaf. Some recipes call for more olives than the ³/₄ cup suggested here. Feel free to experiment, but be careful not to overwhelm the loaf.*

If you have a pizza stone, you might consider making smaller loaves that will fit on the stone. Be sure to put the stone in the oven while it is preheating, and allow extra time for the stone to reach the proper temperature.

FOUGASSE

Yield: 2 flat breads.

1 ½ cups **water**

1 tablespoon **olive oil**

2 teaspoons **salt**

3 cups **HODGSON MILL Best for Bread Flour**

1 cup **HODGSON MILL Whole Wheat Graham Flour**

½ cup **HODGSON MILL Buckwheat Flour**

2 ¼ teaspoons **FLEISCHMANN'S Bread Machine Yeast**

¾ cup coarsely chopped pitted **ripe (black) olives**

1 (2 ¼-ounce) can sliced **ripe (black) olives**, drained (optional)

Add water, oil, salt, bread flour, whole wheat flour, buckwheat flour, yeast and chopped olives to bread machine pan in the order suggested by manufacturer. Select **dough/manual cycle**.

When cycle is complete, remove dough from machine to lightly floured surface. If necessary, knead in enough additional flour to make dough easy to handle. Divide dough in half. Roll each half to ½-inch-thick oval. Place on greased baking sheet. Using a sharp knife, make 4 or 5 parallel slashes, starting about 1 inch from one edge and going across the bread to within 1 inch of the other edge. Pull the slashes apart slightly to enlarge the opening, to accentuate the "ladder" shape. Decorate the tops with sliced olives, if desired. Cover and let rise in a warm, draft-free place about 30 to 45 minutes, or until almost doubled in size.

Bake in a preheated 400-degree oven 25 to 35 minutes, or until done. Remove from pan and let cool on wire racks.

CHALLAH

Yield: 1 large loaf; about 20 to 25 slices.

2 packages **FLEISCHMANN'S Active Dry Yeast**

1 cup lukewarm **water**

1 tablespoon **granulated sugar**

6 to 7 1/2 cups **HODGSON MILL Best for Bread Flour**, divided

1 1/2 cups lukewarm **water**

3/4 cup **vegetable oil**

3 **eggs**, beaten

1/2 cup **granulated sugar**

1 teaspoon **salt**

1 teaspoon **ground cinnamon**

1 tablespoon **vanilla extract**

1 **egg**, beaten, for glaze

Sesame or **poppy seeds** (optional)

Combine yeast, 1 cup lukewarm water and 1 tablespoon sugar in medium bowl; stir to mix. Let stand 5 to 10 minutes, or until foamy. Stir in 2 cups of the flour; let stand about 30 minutes to let the yeast develop.

Combine 1 1/2 cups lukewarm water, oil and 3 eggs in a large bowl; mix well. Stir in 1/2 cup sugar, salt, cinnamon and vanilla. Add the yeast mixture; mix well.

Add the remaining flour, about 1 cup at a time, until you get slightly firm dough. It will be a bit softer than ordinary bread dough because of the eggs. Knead in bowl about 5 minutes. Cover and let rise in warm, draft-free place about 1 1/2 hours, or until doubled in bulk.

Punch down dough. Turn out dough onto a lightly floured surface. Knead briefly to work out the larger air pockets. Divide dough into 3 equal pieces. Roll each piece into a rope, about 24 inches long. Braid ropes to form a loaf, tucking the ends under-

Bread Break

I first made challah when I was a senior in high school, for a cast party on the closing night of *Fiddler on the Roof,* which was our musical that year. It seemed appropriate because challah is traditionally served on the Sabbath, and "Sabbath Prayer" was one of our favorite scenes in the show.

This recipe takes a lot of time and effort, but it's really worth it, if only for the scent of the bread baking. I once made several loaves of challah for community supper, and we could smell it all through evening prayer before the meal. It's now a monastery favorite. It also sells well at Friar Tuck's Bake Shoppe at our drama department's Medieval Faire every year.

neath. Place on a lightly greased baking sheet. Cover with a clean towel and let rise until nearly doubled in bulk. The loaf will be quite large.

About 15 minutes before loaf has finished rising, preheat oven to 375 degrees. Brush loaf all over with beaten egg. Sprinkle with sesame or poppy seeds if desired. Bake about 45 minutes, or until golden brown. If your oven doesn't bake evenly, be sure to turn the pan every 10 minutes or so. Remove loaf from pan and let cool on a rack.

Note: A large, braided loaf is one of the traditional forms of challah. One also finds it shaped as a large braid with a smaller braid on top. I generally prefer to make two smaller single braids, as may be necessary if you have a smaller oven.

CHALLAH

Yield: 1 (2-pound) loaf.

1 1/4 cups **water**

1/4 cup plus 2 tablespoons **vegetable oil**

1 **egg**

1 1/2 teaspoons **vanilla extract**

1 1/2 teaspoons **salt**

3 3/4 cups **HODGSON MILL Best for Bread Flour**

1/4 cup **granulated sugar**

1/2 teaspoon **ground cinnamon**

1 1/2 teaspoons **FLEISCHMANN'S Bread Machine Yeast**

1 **egg**, beaten

Sesame or **poppy seeds** (optional)

Add water, oil, 1 egg, vanilla, salt, flour, sugar, cinnamon and yeast to bread machine pan in the order suggested by manufacturer. Select **dough/manual cycle**.

When cycle is complete, remove dough from machine to a lightly floured surface. If necessary, knead in enough additional flour to make dough easy to handle. Divide dough into 3 equal pieces; roll each piece to 24-inch rope. Braid ropes together, tucking ends underneath. Place on greased baking sheet. Cover; let rise in warm, draft-free place about 1 hour, or until doubled in size. Brush with beaten egg. Sprinkle with sesame or poppy seeds if desired. Bake in a preheated 375-degree oven 35 minutes, or until done. Remove from baking sheet; let cool on wire rack.

Yield: 12 buns.

Bread Break

Hot cross buns are traditional fare for Good Friday and Easter Sunday, but I follow the example of my Grandma Tootsie and serve them several times a year.

Currants are the traditional fruit for hot cross buns, but I much prefer raisins. You will sometimes see hot cross buns with candied orange peel or citron, but they taste too much like fruitcake for me to enjoy them. If you like that sort of thing, reduce the raisins to ¹/₂ cup, and add ¹/₄ cup candied orange peel or other fruitcake-type confection.

Commercial bakeries sometimes omit cutting the cross and simply pipe on some bright yellow frosting — yuck! Don't even think about it!

4 to 4 ¹/₂ cups **HODGSON MILL Best for Bread Flour**, divided

¹/₂ cup **HODGSON MILL Whole Wheat Graham Flour**

1 package **FLEISCHMANN'S Active Dry Yeast**

¹/₄ cup **granulated sugar**

1 ¹/₄ teaspoons **salt**

1 teaspoon **ground cinnamon**

¹/₄ teaspoon **ground nutmeg**

1 cup **milk**

¹/₂ cup (1 stick) **butter**

2 **eggs**, beaten

³/₄ cup **raisins**

VANILLA GLAZE:

³/₄ cup **confectioners' sugar**, sifted

2 tablespoons **milk**

1 tablespoon **butter**, softened

¹/₄ teaspoon **vanilla extract**

Combine 2 cups of the bread flour, whole wheat flour, yeast, sugar, salt, cinnamon and nutmeg in a large bowl; stir until thoroughly blended.

Combine milk and butter in saucepan. Warm over low heat, stirring occasionally, until butter melts. Remove from heat and let cool to lukewarm. Stir in eggs.

Add milk mixture to flour mixture; beat for 200 strokes. Stir in raisins. Add 2 cups bread flour; mix until flour is incorporated. Turn dough out onto a floured surface. Knead lightly, adding enough of the remaining bread flour to make a soft dough that isn't sticky. Knead about 5 minutes, or until dough is smooth and elastic. Lightly rub surface of dough with oil or butter; place in rinsed bowl. Cover and let rise in a warm, draft-free place 1 to 1 ¹/₂ hours, or until doubled in bulk.

Punch down dough and transfer to a floured surface. Knead lightly to remove air bubbles. Divide dough into 12 pieces. Form pieces into balls. Place balls on a lightly greased baking sheet, leaving about 1 inch between balls. Cover with a clean towel and let rise 45 to 60 minutes, or until doubled. Use a sharp knife or razor blade to cut a deep cross in top of each ball.

While dough is rising, preheat oven to 375 degrees. Bake buns 15 to 20 minutes, or until golden. Remove from baking sheet and place on wire rack. Let buns cool 15 minutes.

While buns are cooling, prepare glaze. Combine confectioners' sugar, milk, butter and vanilla in bowl; mix until smooth. Use a pastry brush to apply the glaze to the still-warm buns. Serve warm.

～

Note: *You can make these the night before and they'll still taste fresh in the morning. Measure the vanilla carefully for the glaze. It can easily overwhelm the subtlety of the dough if it is out of proportion with the other flavors.*

HOT CROSS BUNS

Yield: 12 buns.

DOUGH:

1 cup plus 1 tablespoon **milk**

$^1/_2$ cup **butter** or **margarine**

2 **eggs**

1 $^1/_4$ teaspoons **salt**

4 cups **HODGSON MILL Best for Bread Flour**

$^1/_2$ cup **HODGSON MILL Whole Wheat Graham Flour**

$^1/_4$ cup **granulated sugar**

1 teaspoon **ground cinnamon**

$^1/_4$ teaspoon **ground nutmeg**

2 teaspoons **FLEISCHMANN'S Bread Machine Yeast**

$^3/_4$ cup **raisins**

VANILLA GLAZE:

$^3/_4$ cup **confectioners' sugar**, sifted

2 tablespoons **milk**

1 tablespoon **butter**, softened

$^1/_4$ teaspoon **vanilla extract**

Add dough ingredients to bread machine pan in the order suggested by manufacturer. Select **dough/manual cycle**.

When cycle is complete, remove dough from machine to a lightly floured surface. If necessary, knead in enough additional flour to make dough easy to handle. Divide dough into 12 pieces; shape each into a ball. Place balls on greased baking sheet, about 1 inch apart. Cover and let rise in warm, draft-free place about 1 hour, or until doubled in size. With a sharp knife, cut a cross in top of each ball.

Bake in a preheated 375-degree oven 15 minutes, or until done. Remove from baking sheet to wire rack.

Meanwhile, prepare glaze. Combine confectioners' sugar, milk, butter and vanilla in small bowl; stir until smooth. Use a pastry brush to apply glaze to buns while they are still warm.

Specialty Breads

Yield: 2 loaves.

Bread Break

Of all the breads baked during the production of our television show, this bread crumb bread was our director's favorite. The addition of dry bread crumbs gives this loaf a unique flavor and texture, as well as an unusually good crust. The bread crumbs tend to break up the gluten network that holds the dough together, so make sure you add enough flour to make a stiff dough, and knead it thoroughly. Otherwise your dough won't have enough body to hold up during the rising and baking process, and the loaf will collapse as it cools.

1 cup dry **bread crumbs** (see note)

2 cups hot **water**

$^1/_3$ cup **molasses**

3 tablespoons **butter**

2 teaspoons **salt**

2 packages **FLEISCHMANN'S Active Dry Yeast**

$^1/_4$ cup warm **water**

1 tablespoon **HODGSON MILL Vital Wheat Gluten**

1 cup **HODGSON MILL Whole Wheat Graham Flour**

4$^1/_2$ to 5 cups **HODGSON MILL Best for Bread Flour**, divided

Combine bread crumbs, hot water, molasses, butter and salt in a large mixing bowl. Stir until thoroughly blended. Let cool to lukewarm.

Meanwhile, sprinkle yeast over warm water in a small bowl; stir to dissolve. Let stand 5 to 10 minutes, or until foamy.

When bread crumb mixture is lukewarm, add the yeast mixture, gluten and whole wheat flour. Mix thoroughly. Add the bread flour, 1 cup at a time, mixing thoroughly after each addition, until you have a fairly stiff dough.

Turn out dough onto a lightly floured surface and knead 5 minutes. Cover dough and let it rest 5 to 10 minutes. Knead 5 to 7 minutes, incorporating additional flour as needed. The dough will remain slightly sticky but should be quite elastic. Lightly coat the surface of the dough with butter and place in the rinsed mixing bowl. Cover bowl with a clean towel. Let rise in a warm, draft-free place 1 to 1$^1/_2$ hours, or until doubled in bulk.

Punch down dough. Divide dough into two equal pieces and form each piece into a loaf. Place in greased 9x5x3-inch loaf pans. Cover and let rise about 45 minutes, or until nearly doubled.

While dough is rising, preheat oven to 375 degrees. Bake loaves 35 to 45 minutes, or until golden brown. Lightly cover the loaves with aluminum foil if the tops begin to brown too quickly. Loaves are done when they come out of the pan easily and sound hollow when tapped on the bottom. Let cool on wire racks.

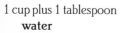

Note: *To make bread crumbs, remove the crusts from stale (but not moldy) bread. Place crusts on an ungreased baking sheet. Bake in a preheated 300-degree oven 10 to 15 minutes; about halfway through, turn them over so they dry evenly. Remove from oven and let cool. Grind dried bread in an electric blender or food processor. If you only have a small amount of bread to crumble, place the dried bread in a plastic bag and crush it with a rolling pin until the crumbs are the desired texture. Dry bread crumbs stored in an airtight container will keep indefinitely.*

BREAD CRUMB BREAD

Bread Machine

Yield: 1 (1 ½-pound) loaf.

1 cup plus 1 tablespoon **water**

3 tablespoons **molasses**

2 tablespoons **butter** or **margarine**

1 teaspoon **salt**

2 cups **HODGSON MILL Best for Bread Flour**

½ cup **HODGSON MILL Whole Wheat Graham Flour**

½ cup dry **bread crumbs**

2 teaspoons **FLEISCHMANN'S Bread Machine Yeast**

1 teaspoon **HODGSON MILL Vital Wheat Gluten**

Add ingredients to bread machine pan in the order suggested by manufacturer. Select **basic cycle; medium/normal color setting**.

Hog Bottom Rolls

Yield: 16 rolls.

Bread Break

I make these rolls at Thanksgiving. One year Father Ronald commented on how one roll quite by accident came out looking like the back end of a pig. With a little experimentation, Hog Bottom Rolls were born!

You can, of course, make traditional crescent rolls with this dough. My brothers and sisters and I loved crescent rolls when we were growing up, and we still do today. We call them "Fred Flintstone Telephone Rolls." They received their name because to us they looked like the telephones on the television show *The Flintstones.* When these rolls were served, it was one of the few times we were allowed to "play with your food." We would pretend to dial the phone and call each other up using the crescent rolls as receivers.

Once when my mom was looking for a recipe for crescent rolls, she searched for an hour in every cookbook without success—

1 package **FLEISCHMANN'S Active Dry Yeast**

$^1/_4$ cup warm **water**

1 (8-ounce) carton **sour cream**

2 tablespoons **solid vegetable shortening**

3 tablespoons **granulated sugar**

$^1/_8$ teaspoon **baking soda**

1 teaspoon **salt**

1 **egg**, beaten

3 cups **HODGSON MILL Naturally White Flour**

Melted **butter** (optional)

Sprinkle yeast over warm water in a small bowl; stir to dissolve. Let stand 5 to 10 minutes, or until foamy.

Combine sour cream, shortening and sugar in a saucepan over medium heat; bring to scalding (just below boiling); do not allow to boil. Stir in baking soda and salt. Let cool to lukewarm.

Pour sour cream mixture into large mixing bowl. Add yeast mixture and egg; mix. Add flour, 1 cup at a time, mixing after each addition. Turn out onto lightly floured surface. Knead about 2 minutes. Cover with a clean towel and let rest about 5 minutes, for the dough to firm up.

Divide dough into 2 equal pieces. Roll each piece into a circle roughly 16 inches in diameter. With a sharp knife, cut 8 wedges from each circle. Starting with the wide end of each triangle (wedge), roll up tightly leaving about 1 inch of the point unrolled. Shape into crescents, making sure the ends of the roll point straight down like the feet of a pig, rather than curving in. Using the blunt side of a butter knife, make a vertical crease in the thick part of the roll.

Twist the unrolled point of
the dough to form the
curly tail and pull it on
top of the crease. Place
rolls on lightly greased
baking sheets. Cover and let
rise in a warm, draft-free place 1 to
1 1/2 hours, or until almost doubled in
size. You may need to gently re-crease the roll after rising.

About 15 minutes before end of rising time, preheat oven to 375
degrees. Bake rolls 12 to 15 minutes, or until golden brown.
Remove from baking sheets and let cool on wire racks. Brush
with melted butter, if desired.

Note: *This dough can be used to make terrific cinnamon rolls.*

because she was looking
under "F"! She had become
so used to the name we had
given them, she had forgot-
ten what everyone else calls
them.

Yield: 16 rolls.

¹/₄ cup **water**

1 (8-ounce) carton
sour cream

2 tablespoons **solid
vegetable shortening**

1 **egg**

1 teaspoon **salt**

3 cups **HODGSON MILL
Best for Bread Flour**

3 tablespoons **granulated sugar**

¹/₈ teaspoon **baking soda**

2 teaspoons **FLEISCHMANN'S
Bread Machine Yeast**

Melted butter (optional)

Add ingredients to bread machine pan in the order suggested by manufacturer. Select **dough/manual cycle**.

When cycle is complete, remove dough from machine to a lightly floured surface. If necessary, knead in enough additional flour to make dough easy to handle. Divide dough in half. Roll each half to 16-inch circle. With sharp knife, cut each circle into 8 wedges. Roll up tightly from wide end leaving about 1 inch of the point unrolled. Shape into crescents, making sure the ends of the roll point straight down like the feet of a pig, rather than curving in. Using the blunt side of a butter knife, make a vertical crease in the thick part of the roll. Twist the unrolled point of the dough to form the curly tail and pull it on top of the crease. Place rolls on greased baking sheets. Cover and let rise in warm, draft-free place 1 to 1¹/₂ hours, or until almost doubled in size. You may need to gently re-crease the roll after rising.

Bake in a preheated 375-degree oven 12 to 15 minutes, or until done. Remove from baking sheets; let cool on wire racks. Brush with melted butter, if desired.

PULL-APART GARLIC BREAD

Yield: 2 (12-serving) loaves.

2 loaves **white bread dough** (your favorite recipe or store-bought)

1/2 cup (1 stick) **butter** or **margarine**, melted (do not use diet spread)

2 tablespoons **dried parsley flakes** or 3 tablespoons fresh

1 tablespoon **Italian herb mix** (see page 100 under Papa Dom's Pizza Topping)

1 tablespoon **granulated garlic** (or more, if stronger garlic flavor is desired)

1 **egg**, beaten (optional)

Grated **Parmesan cheese** (optional)

If using frozen bread dough, let thaw.

Combine melted butter, parsley, Italian herb mix and garlic in a bowl; mix well.

For each loaf, divide dough into 12 pieces. Dip each piece of dough into the butter mixture, coating completely. Arrange 12 pieces in a single layer in each of two greased 9x5x3-inch loaf pans; you'll have to squish the pieces a little to make them fit. Pour any remaining butter mixture over the two loaves. Cover and let rise until dough just reaches the top of the pan.

While dough is rising, preheat oven to 375 degrees. Bake loaves about 45 minutes, or until done. If desired, about 10 minutes before the bread is done, brush the top of each loaf with beaten egg and sprinkle with Parmesan cheese. Remove from pans and serve warm.

~

Note: *Sometimes the butter mixture spills out of the pans, so I set the pans on a rimmed baking sheet to catch any drips. Otherwise you have to clean the bottom of the oven. Also, in an electric oven there can be a danger of fire; this is a matter of personal experience!*

If you have leftovers (not very likely!), reheat in a conventional oven, not in the microwave oven. This is a good general rule for all home-made breads, because the crust gets tough after microwaving.

Bread Break

This bread pulls apart in sections with herbed garlic butter on all sides. Use any white bread dough, even frozen dough from the store. You need enough dough for two loaves.

Our high school's theater production crew—the Stage Rats—really like this bread with Italian beef from the deli at Econo Foods. Each year they eat about six loaves at our Christmas party.

HONEY OATMEAL BREAD

Yield: 2 loaves.

Bread Break

I personally cannot stand oatmeal for breakfast, unlike our Brother Bede, who turns it into a major culinary ritual by baptizing it with milk and anointing it with butter and honey. However, I love oatmeal bread, and the extra oat coating on this bread makes it especially good. The dough will be somewhat stickier than other doughs, so be careful not to add too much flour. This bread is quite chewy, and is excellent toasted. A monastery favorite, it sells quickly at bake sales because of its beautiful appearance.

1 cup **instant oats**, uncooked

2 cups hot **water**

1 package **FLEISCHMANN'S Active Dry Yeast**

$^1/_4$ cup warm **water**

$^1/_3$ cup **honey**

1 tablespoon **butter** or **vegetable oil**

2 teaspoons **salt**

1 **egg**, beaten (optional)

About 5 $^1/_2$ cups **HODGSON MILL Naturally White Flour**, divided

Additional **instant oats**, for coating

Put the oats in a large bowl. Bring 2 cups hot water to a boil; pour it over the oats and let stand at least 15 minutes.

Sprinkle yeast over $^1/_4$ cup warm water in small bowl; stir to mix. Let stand 5 minutes to dissolve.

Feel the oats at the bottom of the bowl to be sure they're lukewarm. Add honey, butter, salt and yeast mixture. For an extra-rich dough, add egg. Mix well. Work in enough of the flour so the dough can be handled, but remember that the oats and honey will make this a very sticky dough.

Turn out dough onto a lightly floured surface. Knead 1 or 2 minutes. Cover and let rest 10 minutes. Knead until dough is elastic but still rather sticky, adding flour as needed; don't add too much flour at a time.

Place dough in a greased bowl and turn to coat. Cover and let rise in a warm, draft-free place about 1 hour, or until doubled in bulk.

Punch down dough and divide into two equal pieces. Knead each piece to remove the large air bubbles. Do not use any flour on the kneading surface; you want the dough to remain sticky. Form each piece into a loaf. Roll each loaf in additional oats until completely covered. Place loaves on lightly greased baking sheets. Cover and let rise about 30 minutes, or until doubled.

While dough is rising, preheat oven to 350 degrees. Bake loaves about 45 minutes, or until they sound hollow when tapped on the bottom. Remove from baking sheets and let cool on wire racks.

Note: *Breads made with honey might darken more quickly during baking than other breads. If the loaves start to get too dark, loosely cover them with aluminum foil and continue baking.*

For an excellent low-fat sandwich, use this bread with garden-fresh tomatoes and smoked turkey. There's no need for cheese or dressing for added flavor.

Honey Oatmeal Bread

Yield: 1 (1 1/2-pound) loaf.

1 cup **water**

3 tablespoons **honey**

1 1/2 teaspoons **butter**

1 teaspoon **salt**

1/2 cup **instant oats**, uncooked

2 1/2 cups **HODGSON MILL Best for Bread Flour**

1 1/2 teaspoons **FLEISCHMANN'S Bread Machine Yeast**

Add ingredients to bread machine pan in the order suggested by manufacturer. Select **basic cycle; medium/color setting.**

Whole Wheat Stuffing Bread

Yield: 2 loaves.

Bread Break

This is the ideal bread for turkey sandwiches the day after a holiday meal. The bread tastes like stuffing!

This was one of my first attempts at herb bread without a net (i.e., with no recipe). I'm happy with the results.

I began herb gardening after reading *The Pleasure of Herbs* by Phyllis Shaudys. In it, she describes how enjoyable it is to bundle up, go outside, brush snow off the sage and thyme, and harvest some to use in stuffing. It sounded so charming I resolved to grow herbs on the spot, and the following Thanksgiving I experienced the pleasure of a winter herb harvest firsthand.

2 packages **FLEISCHMANN'S Active Dry Yeast**

1 cup warm **water**

1 tablespoon **brown sugar**

2 1/2 to 3 cups **HODGSON MILL Best for Bread Flour**, divided

3 tablespoons **vegetable oil**

1/2 cup chopped **onion**

1 tablespoon **dried sage**

2 teaspoons **dried thyme**

1 cup **milk**

2 teaspoons **salt**

2 cups **HODGSON MILL Whole Wheat Graham Flour**

Combine yeast, warm water, brown sugar and 1/2 cup of the bread flour in a bowl; stir to dissolve yeast. Let stand 10 minutes until foamy.

Heat oil in a skillet. Add onion; cook over medium heat and stir until translucent but not browned. Remove from heat. Stir in sage and thyme. Let cool to lukewarm.

Heat milk in a saucepan until lukewarm. Combine milk, onion mixture and salt in a large mixing bowl. Stir in yeast mixture.

Add the whole wheat flour; mix thoroughly. Let rest 5 minutes. Add 2 cups of the bread flour, 1 cup at a time, mixing after each addition. Add enough of the remaining bread flour, 1/4 cup at a time, to make a fairly stiff dough. Turn out dough onto a lightly floured surface. Knead 6 to 8 minutes, or until the dough is smooth, shiny and slightly sticky.

Lightly oil the surface of the dough; place in the rinsed mixing bowl. Cover with a clean towel and let rise in a warm, draft-free place about 1 hour, or until doubled.

Punch down dough. Knead about 1 minute. Divide dough into 2 equal pieces. Form each piece into a loaf and place in greased 9x5x3-inch loaf pans. Or, shape free-form or round loaves and place on a greased baking sheet. Cover and let rise 30 to 45 minutes, or until nearly doubled. If making free-form or round loaves, cut diagonal slashes in the tops with a sharp knife.

While dough is rising, preheat oven to 375 degrees. Bake loaves 45 minutes, or until golden brown and loaves sound hollow when tapped. Remove from pans and let cool on wire racks.

Note: *Be sure your whole wheat flour is fresh. Whole wheat flour can go rancid faster than white flour, and that has a seriously negative effect on the flavor of the bread.*

A tablespoon of wheat gluten added before the flour goes in will make a lighter, softer loaf.

Yield: 2 loaves.

Bread Break

As far as I know, the oldest recorded recipe is found in Ezekiel 4:9, where God tells the prophet, "Take wheat and barley, beans and lentils, millet and spelt; put them in a single vessel and make bread out of them." This prophetic gesture is a sign of the siege of Jerusalem, since under siege conditions wheat flour would be in short supply and other flours would have to be used.

Each of these specialty flours has its unique flavor and texture, and each contains extra nutrients. However, these flours are low in gluten, which means they must be used in combination with wheat flour to achieve a well-risen loaf.

You might have trouble finding barley, millet and spelt flours. Check your local health food store or organic grocery. If you can find pearl barley (which is used in soups and stews), you can grind your own barley flour (see note). Flours from

2 cups warm **water**

2 packages **FLEISCHMANN'S Active Dry Yeast**

2 tablespoons **honey**

¼ cup **vegetable oil**

2 teaspoons **salt**

1½ cups **HODGSON MILL Whole Wheat Graham Flour**, divided

¼ cup **lentil flour**

¼ cup **white bean flour** (fava, navy, etc.)

¼ cup **barley flour**

¼ cup **millet flour**

¼ cup **HODGSON MILL Organic Spelt Flour**

1½ tablespoons **ground coriander**

2 to 2½ cups **HODGSON MILL Best for Bread Flour**

Sesame seeds or **poppy seeds** (optional)

Combine warm water, yeast, honey, oil and salt in a large bowl; stir to dissolve. Stir in ½ cup of the whole wheat flour. Beat thoroughly. Let stand 10 minutes, or until foamy.

Sift the remaining 1 cup whole wheat flour, lentil flour, bean flour, barley flour, millet flour, spelt flour and coriander into a large bowl; stir until well mixed.

Add flour mixture, about 1 cup at a time, to yeast mixture, stirring thoroughly to incorporate each addition. Add enough of the bread flour to make a stiff dough that pulls away from the sides of the bowl.

Turn out dough onto a lightly floured surface. Knead 10 to 12 minutes. Rinse dough bowl and lightly oil the inside. Rub a thin coating of oil on dough and place it in oiled bowl. Cover and let rise in a warm, draft-free place 1½ hours, or until doubled in bulk.

Punch down dough. Knead lightly, then let dough rest 5 minutes. Divide dough into two equal pieces. Form each piece into round loaf. Place loaves on lightly greased baking sheet. Cover and let rise 30 to 45 minutes, or until nearly doubled.

While dough is rising, preheat oven to 350 degrees. If desired, lightly brush tops of risen loaves with water and sprinkle with sesame seeds or poppy seeds. Bake in 350-degree oven about 45 minutes, or until tops are browned and loaves sound hollow when tapped. Remove from baking sheet and let cool on wire racks.

other grains, such as oats, rye or buckwheat, can be substituted, but they are less authentic and will add a different flavor.

⁓

Note: You can make your own bean or grain flours by grinding dried beans or whole grains in an electric blender or food processor. Do not grind more than $1/4$ cup at a time. It will take some time to produce a fine flour, so let the blender rest periodically so it doesn't overheat. Sift the ground mixture through a fine sieve before use, or use a regular flour sifter if you want a coarser blend.

These various flours absorb moisture at different rates, so be sure to follow the directions about sifting them together before adding them to the yeast mixture.

EZEKIEL'S SIX-GRAIN BREAD

Yield: 1 (1½-pound) loaf.

1 cup **water**

2 tablespoons **vegetable oil**

1 tablespoon **honey**

1 teaspoon **salt**

1¼ cups **HODGSON MILL Best for Bread Flour**

¾ cup **HODGSON MILL Whole Wheat Graham Flour**

2 tablespoons **lentil flour**

2 tablespoons **white bean flour**

2 tablespoons **barley flour**

2 tablespoons **millet flour**

2 tablespoons **HODGSON MILL Organic Spelt Flour**

2¼ teaspoons **ground coriander**

2¼ teaspoons **FLEISCHMANN'S Bread Machine Yeast**

Sesame or **poppy seeds**

Add ingredients (except sesame seeds) to bread machine pan in the order suggested by manufacturer. Select **dough/manual cycle**.

When cycle is complete, remove dough from machine to a lightly floured surface. If necessary, knead in enough additional flour to make dough easy to handle. Shape dough into a ball; place on greased baking sheet. Cover and let rise in a warm, draft-free place about 45 minutes, or until doubled in size. Lightly brush top of loaf with water; sprinkle with sesame or poppy seeds.

Bake in a preheated 350-degree oven 25 to 30 minutes, or until done. Remove from baking sheet; let cool on wire rack.

Pizza Plus

PIZZA DOUGH

Yield: Enough dough for 2 large thick-crust pizzas or 3 large thin-crust pizzas.

Bread Break

Every Thursday night, except during Lent, the monks at St. Bede have what we call a "haustus," which comes from the Latin *hausere*, meaning "to be filled or satisfied." Haustus is a community night when the brothers gather for a couple of hours of conversation, card playing, board games and so forth. And what's a card party without food? Brother Bede and Brother Luke always make a huge batch of popcorn. There's usually a tray of salami, sliced ham, cheese and sometimes leftover cold chicken for sandwiches. And once or twice a month, I make homemade pizza. I usually make this dough after school at 3:00 p.m. I let it rise once, punch it down and let it rise a second time in the refrigerator until after evening prayer, when haustus begins.

1 package **FLEISCHMANN'S Active Dry Yeast**

1 tablespoon **brown sugar**

³/₄ cup **HODGSON MILL Whole Wheat Graham Flour**

2 cups lukewarm **water**

¹/₄ cup **olive oil**

1 tablespoon **salt**

4¹/₂ to 5 cups **HODGSON MILL Naturally White Flour**, divided

Combine yeast, brown sugar and the whole wheat flour in a large bowl; mix thoroughly. Add water; stir until well mixed. Let yeast develop about 15 minutes. (During this time you can be chopping vegetables or browning sausage for your pizza topping.)

Add oil and salt to yeast mixture; mix well. Add 2 cups of the white flour; beat for 200 strokes. Add 2 cups white flour; beat another 200 strokes. Add enough of the remaining white flour to make a stiff dough. Knead about 8 minutes. Place dough in an oiled bowl and turn to coat. Cover and let rise in a warm, draft-free place about 1 hour, or until doubled in bulk.

Punch down dough. Knead one minute. Return dough to bowl. Cover top with plastic wrap. Refrigerate up to 4 hours.

Remove dough from the fridge about 30 minutes before you're going to use it. Divide dough into 2 or 3 equal portions. Roll each portion out to the size of your pan; a heavier-gauge pizza pan is recommended. Prick the crust all over with a fork or other tool (I use an angel food cake cutter). This pricking keeps the dough from inflating like a pita pocket in the oven.

Top with your favorite ingredients (see page 100 for Papa Dom's Pizza Topping). Bake in a preheated 400-degree oven 15 to 20 minutes or until crust begins to brown.

Note: If you're not going to need this much dough, use the remainder to make focaccia, an Italian hearth bread (see page 70).

You can use the dough after the first rising, but the quality of the crust will be much better if the dough gets a second slow rising in the fridge. The olive oil makes a big difference, too, as does the use of a baking stone.

For thick crusts, I usually roll out the dough and bake it for 5 or 10 minutes before I add any toppings. This seals the crust and keeps it from getting soggy.

VARIATION
Follow the recipe above. After the yeast mixture develops, add oil, salt (reduce amount to 2 teaspoons), 1/4 cup chopped fresh Italian herbs (basil, rosemary, marjoram, chives, thyme, etc.) and 1/4 cup grated Parmesan cheese. Proceed as directed.

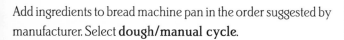
PIZZA DOUGH

Bread Machine

Yield: Enough dough for one 12-inch pizza.

1 cup **water**	1 1/2 teaspoons **brown sugar**
2 tablespoons **olive oil**	1 1/2 teaspoons
1 1/2 teaspoons **salt**	**FLEISCHMANN'S Bread Machine Yeast**
2 1/2 cups **HODGSON MILL Best for Bread Flour**	

Add ingredients to bread machine pan in the order suggested by manufacturer. Select **dough/manual cycle**.

When cycle is complete, remove dough from machine; place in oiled bowl and turn to coat. Cover with plastic wrap; refrigerate for up to 4 hours. Remove from the refrigerator about 30 minutes before using. Proceed as directed in traditional recipe.

PAPA DOM'S PIZZA TOPPING

Yield: Enough topping for 2 medium pizzas.

Bread Break

If you don't much care for tomato sauce, or if you just prefer something a little different from the usual sausage and pepperoni, try this vegetarian pizza topping. Pair it with mozzarella cheese for a great pizza.

When I make pizza for the monks, I often invite some students from our high school to help. Surprisingly, even kids who have been raised on delivery pizza absolutely love this topping.

If there is any topping left over, add it to a salad the next day. You also can use this flavorful topping on wheat crackers or garlic toast as an appetizer.

4 large **plum tomatoes**

1 small **onion**

4 cloves **garlic**

8 **Kalamata** or **Greek olives**

3 tablespoons grated **Asiago cheese**

2 tablespoons **olive oil**

1 tablespoon **Italian herb mix** (see note)

Cut tops off tomatoes. Squeeze out and discard juice and seeds. Dice remaining tomato pulp; place in bowl. Chop onion; you should get about ¼ cup. Add onion to tomatoes. Mince garlic; add to bowl along with herbs. Pit and chop olives; add to bowl. Add cheese and oil. Mix well. Cover and refrigerate until ready to use.

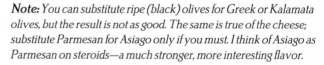

Note: You can substitute ripe (black) olives for Greek or Kalamata olives, but the result is not as good. The same is true of the cheese; substitute Parmesan for Asiago only if you must. I think of Asiago as Parmesan on steroids—a much stronger, more interesting flavor.

Use any Italian herb mix you like, commercial or homemade. Here's the one I prefer:

Italian Herb Mix

2 parts dried rosemary
2 parts dried basil
2 parts dried parsley flakes

1 part dried thyme
1 part dried marjoram
½ part dried sage

Combine herbs in jar with airtight lid. Store at room temperature. Shake well before using.

The flavor of this herb mix is better if you make it at least two hours ahead and let the various elements blend.

Turkey Sausage

Yield: About 2 pounds sausage.

1 pound **ground turkey**

1 pound **garlic pork sausage**

1 tablespoon **Italian herb mix** (page 100)

1 tablespoon **garlic powder**

1 tablespoon **anise seeds**

1 teaspoon **crushed red pepper**

1 teaspoon **paprika**

1 teaspoon **celery salt**

¹/₂ teaspoon **black pepper**

¹/₂ teaspoon **white pepper**

¹/₂ teaspoon **salt**

Combine ground turkey, sausage, Italian herb mix, garlic powder, anise seeds, crushed red pepper, paprika, celery salt, black pepper, white pepper and salt in large bowl. Mix thoroughly. Cover and refrigerate until ready to use as a pizza topping.

Note: *The flavors in the sausage are best if you let it sit in the refrigerator for a few hours before you cook it. I generally brown this sausage in a cast-iron skillet one pound at a time and drain it thoroughly before using it on pizza. Because 2 pounds is a lot unless you're feeding a huge crowd, you can halve the recipe, or brown the whole batch and freeze half for up to one month.*

This sausage may be used in spaghetti sauce, too.

Bread Break

We have a number of monks who are on restricted diets, so I developed this recipe for reduced-fat sausage. Besides the half pork/half turkey version given here, you can make it entirely from turkey, but the change in flavor and texture is really noticeable.

I use mozzarella cheese made from part skim milk, and turkey pepperoni, so my pizzas are more healthful than most. Nonetheless, my confrere Brother Michael was distressed to learn that he had been eating turkey, because he'd been limiting himself to one or two pieces of pizza, not even knowing he had been getting a reduced-fat snack!

Bread Break

Even though the monks of my community eat a *lot* of bread, there are always some leftovers. Crostini are a fast and easy way to use up the tail end of a baguette or other crusty loaf. One morning I saw that we were going to have leftover spaghetti for lunch, so I used a day-old hero sandwich loaf to make garlic and cheese crostini. As I brought them into the dining room, Abbot Roger grinned and said, "I was hoping someone would think of that!"

Use leftover baguette bread (the long, skinny loaves, or the shape used for submarine sandwiches). Cut the bread into slices 1/2 inch thick. Place slices on an ungreased baking sheet. Bake in a preheated 350-degree oven 15 to 20 minutes, turning once, or until crostini are crisp and slightly browned.

Crostini can be used as a base for appetizers of various kinds. Try sprinkling crostini with cheese and herbs and putting them under the broiler until the cheese melts.

Instead of serving packaged crackers with salad, serve crostini that have been rubbed with a freshly cut garlic clove or brushed with a flavored olive oil.

I like to serve crostini with Papa Dom's Pizza Topping (page 100) as antipasto. Just put a bowl of the topping in the middle of a flat basket filled with crostini, and your party is off to a great start!

CROUTONS

Preheat oven to 350 degrees. Use leftover slices of bread that are stale but not moldy or excessively dry. Remove the crusts, then cut the bread into cubes about $1/2$ inch square. Place the bread cubes in a roasting pan. Drizzle on 2 or 3 tablespoons of melted butter or olive oil, then toss the mixture so the cubes are lightly coated. Use more oil or butter if you are making a large batch, but remember that the idea is to coat the croutons lightly, not soak them in grease. If you want flavored croutons, you may mix in finely chopped herbs or minced garlic as well. Place the pan in the oven and bake, stirring the croutons every 5 minutes; 15 minutes is long enough for lightly toasted croutons, 30 minutes if you want them a bit drier. Serve on top of soups or salads.

Note: *Unlike the commercial, dry-as-dust, hard-as-rocks variety, homemade croutons are best if they are made just before use. But you can also make them a few hours ahead of time and store them in an airtight container at room temperature. Just before you are going to serve them, you might re-crisp the croutons on a baking sheet in a 350-degree oven for 5 minutes.*

Bread Break

I don't care for commercial croutons—they're too salty, rock hard, and the edges are so sharp they scratch the roof of my mouth, which does nothing to improve the experience of eating salad. Homemade croutons are fast and easy, and you can make them as crisp or as soft as you like. When you are entertaining, homemade croutons are one of those little touches that show you really care about your guests.

Bread Break

These herb spreads can be prepared a day or two before use, which allows the flavors to blend thoroughly. I use these spreads to make an easy-to-prepare snack when I invite friends for tea. I make a quick batch of Sweet Cornmeal Muffins (page 20) and one or two herb spreads, put the kettle on, and I'm ready for a party!

SWEET BLEND:

1 cup (2 sticks) **butter**, softened

¹/₄ cup **honey**

1 teaspoon **ground coriander**

¹/₄ teaspoon **dried thyme**

1 tablespoon chopped **fresh lemon balm**

Makes about 1 ¹/₄ cups.

LIGHT BLEND:

1 cup (2 sticks) reduced-fat **margarine** or **vegetable oil spread**, softened

1 tablespoon chopped **fresh sage**

1 tablespoon chopped **fresh chives**

Makes about 1 cup.

ITALIAN CREAM CHEESE:

12 ounces **cream cheese** (four 3-ounce packages), softened

1 teaspoon **dried basil**

1 teaspoon **dried marjoram**

1 tablespoon **dried parsley flakes**

1 teaspoon **granulated garlic**

Makes about 1 ¹/₂ cups.

For each of the spreads: Combine the softened butter (or margarine or cream cheese) with the other ingredients in a medium bowl; mix thoroughly. Cover and refrigerate up to two days before use. Use as a spread for bread or crackers.

POTENZA MEATBALLS

Yield: About 16 large or 32 small meatballs.

2 pounds **ground beef chuck**

2 cups **fresh bread crumbs**

1 **egg**

3 small cloves **garlic**, crushed

3 tablespoons **dried parsley flakes**

1 tablespoon **dried oregano**

1 tablespoon **dried basil**

3 tablespoons grated **Romano cheese**

Combine beef, bread crumbs, egg, garlic, parsley, oregano, basil and cheese in a large mixing bowl. Thoroughly mix ingredients by hand. Form mixture into meatballs, pressing firmly to make sure they stay together. Make petite meatballs for soup, larger ones for spaghetti.

Brown meatballs in a skillet over medium heat, turning occasionally, until thoroughly cooked. Drain off grease before adding meatballs to spaghetti sauce or soup.

Bread Break

I normally prefer to use fresh herbs in my cooking, but I got this recipe with dried herbs from Grandpa Garramone, who got it from Great-Grandma Fiori, so I don't want to mess with it! That side of my family came from Potenza on the west coast of Italy, hence the name.

I know from personal experience that cold meatballs with a bit of spaghetti sauce make the best sandwich for a sack lunch that an Italian kid could hope for. In a pinch, meatballs make a pretty good breakfast, too!

Yield: 6 servings.

Bread Break

All Friday meals in the monastery are meatless, so coming up with flavorful vegetarian dishes is a challenge. One afternoon, Helen, one of the cooks on our kitchen staff, developed this delicious meatless chili. It was a huge hit, and I coaxed the recipe out of her after supper.

This chili soup is not quite as thick as regular chili, but it's just as delicious. For a great Lenten lunch, serve chili soup with grilled Cheddar cheese sandwiches or Southwest Cornmeal Muffins (see page 73).

---

¹/₂ pound **dried kidney beans**

¹/₂ pound **dried pinto beans**

Water

6 to 8 cups **boiling water**

3 cloves **garlic**, minced

1 large **onion**, diced

1 **bay leaf**

¹/₄ teaspoon **dried thyme**

¹/₂ teaspoon **dried marjoram**

1 cup **vegetable broth**

1 (15- or 16-ounce) can **tomatoes**, undrained (2 cups)

1 cup **tomato juice** (in addition to juice from tomatoes)

¹/₂ cup **brown rice**, uncooked

1 ¹/₄ teaspoons **cayenne pepper**

1 teaspoon **chili powder**

Rinse beans. Put in large soup pot and add water to cover. Let stand about one hour. Drain beans into a colander; rinse beans and pot.

Return beans to pot. Add boiling water, garlic, onion, bay leaf, thyme and marjoram. Cover and simmer 1 to 2 hours, or until beans are cooked. Check occasionally and add water as needed to keep beans from cooking dry.

Add broth, tomatoes with their juice, tomato juice, brown rice, cayenne and chili powder. Cover and simmer one hour, or until chili is of desired thickness. Remove and discard bay leaf. Serve chili hot.

≈

Note: *Unlike most chili, this recipe is better the first day, so make it fresh. For vegetable broth, use vegetable bouillon cubes or granules or make it from scratch.*

Rather than soaking and cooking dry beans, you may prefer using canned beans. If so, substitute 2 (15- or 16-ounce) cans kidney beans, undrained, and 1 (15- or 16-ounce) can pinto beans, undrained. Combine beans, garlic, onion, bay leaf, thyme, marjoram, broth, tomatoes with their juice, tomato juice, brown rice, cayenne and chili powder in pot. Add water as needed for desired consistency. Cover and simmer 1 hour.

TV Series Episodes

Illustrations

Refer to these illustrations to find out how to do basic techniques for many of the recipes mentioned in this book.

Bread Machine Recipes

General Index